D1330651

Stakeknife

BRITAIN'S SECRET AGENTS
IN IRELAND

Martin Ingram & Greg Harkin

THE O'BRIEN PRESS
DUBLIN

First published 2004 by The O'Brien Press Ltd,
20 Victoria Road, Dublin 6, Ireland.
Tel: +353 1 4923333; Fax: +353 1 4922777
E-mail: books@obrien.ie
Website: www.obrien.ie

ISBN: 0-86278-843-9

British Library Cataloguing-in-Publication Data
A catalogue record for this title is available from the British Library

1 2 3 4 5 6 7 8 9 10
04 05 06 07 08

Editing, typesetting, layout and design: The O'Brien Press Ltd
Printing: Nørhaven Paperback A/S

Acknowledgements
The authors wish to thank everyone who cooperated in any way in the writing
of this book. Many of them, for security reasons, do not want to be named. They
know who they are. We would particularly like to thank the O'Brien Press for
their courageous approach to this book.

Contents

Introduction: Martin Ingram **page 7**

Introduction: Greg Harkin **14**

Chapter 1: Inside the Force Research Unit – *Ingram* **21**

Chapter 2: Recruiting and Running an Agent – *Ingram* **34**

Chapter 3: Human Intelligence – *Ingram* **50**

Chapter 4: The Agent Stakeknife – *Ingram* **60**

Chapter 5: Fear and Hypocrisy: The Nutting Squad – *Ingram/Harkin* **95**

Chapter 6: Murders in the Republic and Northern Ireland – *Harkin/Ingram* **111**

Chapter 7: 'Get Danny Morrison' – *Harkin* **136**

Chapter 8: The Real Brian Nelson – *Harkin* **160**

Chapter 9: A Litany of Death: Agent 6137 – *Harkin/Ingram* **174**

Chapter 10: The Murder of Pat Finucane – *Harkin* **194**

Chapter 11: Collusion and Conspiracy – *Ingram* **209**

Chapter 12: Notorantonio: The Watershed – *Harkin* **215**

Chapter 13: Double Standards: The Use and Abuse of Agents – *Ingram/Harkin* **227**

Chapter 14: Face-to-Face with Scappaticci – *Harkin* **241**

Chapter 15: Fallout for a Whistleblower – *Ingram* **255**

Glossary 265

Introduction

Martin Ingram

This book is about secrets, secrets the British Ministry of Defence (MOD) would prefer were not made public. But some secrets are too serious to keep under wraps. Some need to be exposed so that such things will never happen again.

In discussing the secret matters in this book the reader will continually demand evidence. The evidence I bring to this book is my own history, my activities within the Force Research Unit (FRU), the unit set up to handle agents and double agents in the context of conflict in Northern Ireland. I spent seven years working for the FRU in Northern Ireland. We were a small, tight-knit bunch in the FRU. We worked together, drank together, played football together. We were each other's support system. Inevitably we talked about our work though each case was meant to be kept secret. My many conversations with my colleagues led me to know the details of most of the cases being handled by the unit. Usually, several of us worked with each agent as this eliminated problems if someone needed to be moved suddenly for security or other reasons. This is the background I bring to this book.

The book is confessional in nature. It is with the intention of speaking out for the sake of a better future that I am revealing things I came across in my work within intelligence-gathering. Certain activities of the FRU have sickened me. I want them aired in public. I feel this is right and necessary. I bring an insider's perspective to bear on situations and incidents tracked and written about by many others. I am simply adding the authenticity of that insider knowledge, adding weight and personal experience, which increases the weight of evidence to the claims of others.

The MOD employs people whose only role in life is to make sure that information released to the media is controlled. For my part I believe genuine secrets deserve to be protected, acquiescence in murder does not.

This book is the culmination of a number of years' work, work which is to be ended once I have promoted this book. Not because the job is finished, because clearly it is not, but because I made a solemn promise to my wife two years ago that normality would be returned to our lives once this book was published. This means no more helping so-called police inquiries, like Stevens 3, Bloody Sunday or Barron, or indeed any other inquiries which may or may not be established in the future. All contact with the media will also be stopped, except where a genuine friendship has been built with a journalist.

My wife, who herself is a nationalist from a deeply republican family, has been a pillar of strength and support. However, even her patience was tested when our home was broken into a number of years ago, and an early working manuscript for this book was taken. It was, within days, being presented to a High Court hearing in London with the aim of securing a conviction against me under the draconian Official Secrets Act. Thankfully, that action failed due in no small part to my brilliant lawyer Peter Binning and to the *Sunday Times* newspaper, which graciously and unwaveringly funded that legal advice.

My wife was incandescent with rage at the audacity of the British; she could not believe the lengths that a government will go to. The Irish Government was informed of these developments through the good offices of Jane Winters, Director of British Irish Rights Watch and a trusted confidant. The Irish Government, who granted me Irish citizenship some years ago, were, to their credit, willing to raise the matter immediately at an intergovernmental meeting. I declined that offer, principally out of self-interest – the circle of knowledge regarding Martin Ingram's place of residence is restricted, and I am very aware that the British Government really does not consider the sovereignty of the Irish state to be of any great significance. So what was there to be gained, except to place overt pressure on the fledgling peace process and highlight my vulnerability? A compliant newspaper in the UK has since published the fact that I reside within the Irish state – for what reason, I will leave the public to decide. My promise to my wife will be honoured, unless the British state increases the stakes and continues to pursue an action in respect of any allegations of breaches of the Official Secrets Act. I believe that the disclosures contained in this book are in the public interest.

The first steps towards this book can be traced to a phone call I made in 1999 to Liam Clarke, a journalist with the *Sunday Times*. This call was in response to an article Liam had written regarding the RUC and its involvement in the murder of the Belfast solicitor Patrick Finucane. We decided to write some articles together. Liam and the *Sunday Times* were viewed with more than a degree of suspicion by the republican community and initially the early articles written under my pseudonym, Martin Ingram, were viewed with much scepticism by them. It was not until both Liam and I were arrested by the British Special Branch for alleged offences under the Official Secrets Act that the scepticism waned. Today, I believe, republicans, both mainstream and dissidents, know that Martin Ingram is being truthful when he maintains that the British State organised and participated in state-sponsored murder; they accept that he believes passionately that those acts were wrong and that we must all help expose those crimes in order to learn from the mistakes of the past. The Unionist community was and remains dismissive.

I have written numerous articles over the years published in the *Guardian*, *Irish News*, *Andersonstown News* and elsewhere, but this is the first time I have had the space to give my whole story.

Obviously people will be suspicious of a whistleblower and I perfectly understand that suspicion. On entering this arena I was like a lost lamb, just feeling my way and trying to help clarify certain issues. I honestly had no intention of staying in this role for any length of time. In hindsight that was a poor judgement call. Unfortunately the MOD raised the stakes: through the State's Treasury Solicitor they applied and were granted an *ex parte* injunction against me under my real name, not my pseudonym, Martin Ingram. This injunction was gained without my knowledge. To be honest, that one act alone galvanised me into taking on the system and confirmed me in my conviction that it was worthwhile exposing what I know about certain incidents. At that moment I decided to stick it out, however difficult it might become. My reaction to the injunction was a mixture of petulance and anger at the audacity of the State to try to control information which, frankly, was of limited value to any potential enemy of the State.

I did take a vow of secrecy when joining the intelligence services. How can I now justify breaking that vow? I justify it by several things: I believe it is vital that certain activities from the war period are brought into the open if the ongoing discussions which are part of the peace process are to succeed. I hope that process will succeed. I believe that the South African experience in which the truth commissions helped clear the air were very valuable and that in order to move on with their lives people need to deal with their past. This, it seems to me, is a good model for resolving problems. But to deal with the past you need to know what that past *actually* involved. There are many unanswered questions, many rumours and counter-rumours. I feel that I have a fairly unique perspective and that I can genuinely help in that resolution so that we can all put our past behind us. I want to help clarify as much as possible, now, so that people can finally get ahead with their futures. I feel justified too because I find that the MOD have been overprotective and in my opinion somewhat paranoid about their activities. They too need to admit what happened, punish whoever deserves it and move on. We have all been too long under the yoke of claim and counterclaim and hidden, dangerous secrets. I am personally sick of that attitude and I genuinely believe that my whistleblowing is helpful. If people disagree with me, then so be it. My commitment is now to the future, not to the past.

The first article published in the *Sunday Times* dealt with the decision of the FRU to play God with the life of Gerry Adams. The article recounted the operation that had been undertaken by the security forces to render the bullets used in the attack as ineffectual. The Treasury Solicitor immediately wrote to the *Sunday Times* and informed them that 'they were satisfied that the newspaper was speaking to someone who had genuine access' and in future they should submit any further material from this source (me – Ingram) prior to publication. Quite rightly the *Sunday Times* refused. In relation to that article, there was little or no prospect of any damage. I believe the public have a right to know how its security and intelligence apparatus was willing to engage in playing God with people's lives.

I lay my cards clearly and openly on the table here. I am convinced that Republicans/ Nationalists were dealt a very strange and unequal deck of cards in Northern Ireland. It is probably inevitable that in a war situation the lines between the moral and the immoral become increasingly murky as the war goes on; over thirty years moral issues will become multilayered and very murky indeed. This is a tricky area for the State to handle. Intelligence activities of their nature deal with people who are treading along very unacceptable paths and the handlers of such agents need to work alongside this. Those in authority need to have strict standards and they need to stick to them. They also need to review them on an ongoing basis. Above all, what I do not accept is that the State whose services I was involved with was completely one-sided. This gradually became clear to me over my time in Northern Ireland, and I find it totally unacceptable. The State was not just an arbitrator, a peacekeeper, it became a participant on the loyalist side.

I now hope to see a free, democratic and united Ireland in my lifetime. I would not be prepared to fight for one because as an Englishman it is clearly not my war to wage. What I can do, though, is inform those who are prepared to listen to an ex-intelligence officer who believes the truth should win out. Much has been written of the violence waged by Republicans and Loyalists during the troubles. This book is different in that it turns over the flip side of the coin: how the State was prepared through its network of agents and agencies to get involved in and even promote a terrorist campaign. It makes for painful reading.

Introduction

Greg Harkin

When Martin Ingram first contacted me over three years ago now, I was at first sceptical about his motivations, his reasons for becoming a whistleblower who is now despised by British Army Intelligence. I would, through time, learn of those reasons: that he had difficulty moving on in his new civilian lifestyle with knowledge of crimes committed by colleagues during what we now call, rather shamefully in my opinion, the Troubles. Three and a half thousand people died during the past thirty-five years and ten times that number suffered some sort of physical injury. Perhaps all of us who live in Northern Ireland have suffered mental scars from existing in a society where intolerance and bigotry is rife.

This book does not set out to address the issues surrounding all those deaths and injuries. The only book that successfully does that is *Lost Lives*, where the death of each individual is dealt with. It is a shocking book. Rather, this book shines a light on how the British Government, through its security agencies, was itself involved in the murder of its own citizens. In the past, loyalist and republican paramilitaries have been collectively blamed for the conflict in Northern Ireland. While there is no doubting their contribution to the endless bloodletting in the name of God, Ulster and Ireland, another contributor to deaths and destruction has been British Government policy. This book does not examine the role of the SAS or any other British Army unit involved in attacks on paramilitaries. That has been done many times before. This book examines the real dirty war in Northern Ireland

and how security force agencies used informers and agents to, at worst, kill, or, at best, allow killings to take place.

It seems that not a month now passes in Northern Ireland without some new allegation surfacing about security-force agents being involved in murder. One report recently said a UVF informer had thirteen murder victims to his credit, all apparently carried out whilst he was a paid agent. I know of another IRA informer who took part in a similar number of killings. These sorts of allegations are rarely investigated properly. When one looks at the clear-up rate for killing, the number of people convicted in contrast to the number of deaths leaves you with the distinct impression that not everything was done to bring those responsible before the courts. I believe this, in part, is because there were so many informers operating inside paramilitary groups that to have properly investigated murders would have led to the detention of those very agents.

There will be those who will attack this book for failing to address the issues surrounding murders carried out by paramilitaries. This is, in fact, precisely what we are doing. Victims of agents include people from all walks of life: IRA members, loyalist paramilitaries, civilians *and* members of the security forces. That is what this book is about – agents who killed, civil servants who murdered for and on behalf of the security forces and the State.

Martin Ingram gives powerful testimony. He first began to seriously question what the Force Research Unit (FRU) did in Northern Ireland after a day out shopping with his wife and young daughter. Not being the shopping type he wandered into a bookshop and began flicking through the book *Killing Rage* by the former IRA member Eamon Collins. He bought it. Later that week he read through the chapter on the Nutting Squad – the IRA's internal security department, so-called because of their practice of 'nutting', ie, putting a bullet through the head of their victims – and saw how 'Scap' and John Joe Magee had joked about the killing of an alleged informer. It left him feeling sick to the pit of his stomach. Ingram knew the 'Scap' referred to was Freddie Scappaticci, but more importantly, that Scappaticci was Stakeknife, an agent run by his former friends in the FRU. When he began to speak out, firstly in the *Sunday Times*, the full might of the law in the UK was used against him and the journalist Liam Clarke. Ingram's home was later burgled and notes for this book stolen. At last, however, this book has made it into print.

We have set out to look at three important areas. Firstly Ingram details how the FRU worked and how agents were recruited and widely used in the conflict in Northern Ireland. (A fellow handler once told me that in Derry city alone one in six IRA volunteers worked for the FRU. This did not include the coverage obtained by the RUC.) Ingram's account is the first time a former member of the security forces has revealed in detail how its intelligence operations worked. The rest of the book is centred around two of the FRU's most important agents inside paramilitary groups.

The first is Freddie Scappaticci. There are still some within republicanism who believe Stakeknife was not a person but the codeword for all intelligence-gathering operations inside the IRA. This is not the case. Scappaticci was given the code-word Steak Knife after his recruitment into the FRU. He was also referred to as Stakeknife and Stake Knife. The spelling would vary depending on the handlers. We have chosen the spelling 'Stakeknife' because it was the one most commonly used. As Ingram says, the IRA leadership made the fatal mistake when hunting for informers in believing that someone who killed on behalf of the Provisional IRA could not possibly be used as an informer. What we now know is that many agents did kill and perhaps none of them was more prolific than Freddie Scappaticci. Infiltrating the very unit set up to provide internal security for the IRA was a master-stroke. It would give the British side coverage they had only previously dreamed of. It would also, however, lead to a change in any morals the British Government would claim to have in its war on republicans. As Ingram has said, there were no rules and there were no borders. Freddie Scappaticci himself would go on to suffer severe depression and other mental illnesses. He is a man who is finding it hard to live with the person he once was – an informer who was literally allowed to get away with murder and the murder of his fellow IRA members. His role cannot be defended. If an agent saves lives then there is justification. But if an agent takes lives while saving other lives then that is totally indefensible. Scap's role will make for painful reading, especially for the families of his victims.

The other significant FRU agent is Brian Nelson. Nelson, a man convicted of a brutal sectarian attack on a partially disabled family man, infiltrated the UDA, but, rather than save lives as an agent, instead he contributed to dozens of sectarian attacks. In conversations with fellow FRU officers, Ingram discovered that Nelson was being used as an extension of the British Army's secret war on the Provisional IRA. While Nelson's role has been covered on many occasions, this is the first time a former FRU handler has given details from within the security forces. It shows the extent to which some Army officers were prepared to go in the dirty war. Innocent people, including the solicitor Pat Finucane, would lose their lives as a result.

During a speech on the IRA, the former UK prime minister, Margaret Thatcher, once famously told the House of Commons that 'murder is murder is murder'. There was no other way to describe deaths carried out by paramilitaries, she said. Yet British agents in Northern Ireland were also carrying out such murders. After you've read this book her speech will never have sounded so hollow.

✳ ✳ ✳

When my newspaper, the *People,* first reported on the Stakeknife story in August/September 2000 an injunction was served on us to prevent any further exposure of this whole story. The paper remains the subject of severe legal restrictions in identifying or reporting on agents or handlers in the FRU. The *People* got support from all sides, with both unionists and nationalists condemning the gagging orders. Stephen McCabe MP, a member of the Northern Ireland Select Committee, said: 'We should not be gagging stories just because they are embarrassing to the government.' British Labour veteran Tony Benn added: 'A government should not suppress news stories.' Northern Ireland loyalists joined the call for the lifting of the gag and demanded that the government explain its reasons for silencing Northern Ireland's Newspaper of the Year.

The allegations cut right across the divide, concerning as they did the horrible murders of both Protestant and Catholic people. The PUP's Billy Hutchinson, MLA said: 'I am concerned about what this means for the freedom of the press. In Northern Ireland we should be investigating what happened in the past. This story should be allowed to run without the government bringing out injunctions.' DUP justice spokesman Ian Paisley Jr said: 'I think the government should answer the questions being put to them. They should explain why they wanted this injunction because it seems that it is in the public interest to say that. It's for the Ministry of Defence to comment on the substance of the allegations, not just to bring an injunction. The reasons for it must be explained.' He said the government should 'change tack and defend its position'. Ex-Ulster Unionist MP Jeffrey Donaldson (who joined the Democratic Unionist party in January 2004) has also said the issue raises fundamental questions concerning press freedom. He said the move was out of step with 'press freedoms granted in a democratic country'. He added: 'Clearly there are times when national security must come first, but I feel this has been abused by the authorities at times. We have to establish where the line is drawn between freedom of the press and national interest'. Sinn Féin and SDLP spokespeople also condemned the government's actions. And Jane Winter, director of London-based British/Irish Rights Watch, said that the British Government was curbing fundamental press freedom. 'The government is prohibiting people from doing their job,' she said. 'They would be better advised in addressing the issues that journalists are trying to raise and perhaps putting some of their energies into respecting the right of the family of Mr Notorantonio to finally know the truth of what happened to him. Freedom of the press is one of the most fundamental aspects of life in any developed democracy. I understand that the terms of this injunction are not even allowed to be discussed. This is ridiculous. I have long been aware of the many allegations involving the Army's Force Research Unit in the eighties and nineties and these are not just going to go away until this matter is addressed.'

The *People* fought back. The then editor Neil Wallis said: 'I was furious. It is amazing that the government and security services can gag what is supposed to be a free press. If they thought we would accept this, they were quite wrong. I told the [British] government they had a real fight on their hands. I was very pleased both the *Sunday People* and the company stood up to the full force of the government machine, including armies of lawyers and MI5 agents. The government initially obtained the most wide-ranging and draconian order imaginable and we weren't even allowed to be present in court. That order has now been shot to pieces.' Most of the terms of the injunction have now been lifted, albeit with a coda that insists that any proposed attempt to identify or investigate agents or handlers has to be submitted, in writing, to the MOD three days prior to publication for approval!

Chapter 1

Inside the Force Research Unit

Ingram

My path to involvement in the British Army's Intelligence Corps, and subsequently in FRU, was not a straightforward one. In fact, I had no ambitions to become a member of the intelligence services at all, but the Army seemed to know from the beginning that this was where I belonged.

Having had a normal, North of England upbringing in a family that was nominally Protestant, and a school career that was more sports-dominated than academically distinguished, I determined, at the age of seventeen to join the Army. I filled in the application forms, but chickened out at the last minute. Although my father was convinced that I was made for Army life, in truth I was probably too immature at that stage. For two years I worked in a variety of jobs, but the 'call' was still there, and at nineteen I took the plunge and walked into my local Army Careers information office.

What did I hope to get out of the Army? Probably an extension of school life: plenty of sport, good fun, a bit of adventure, and I would be paid for it as well. The careers officer recognised my motivation straight away and reassured me that sport played a pivotal role in Army life. The entrance exam was straightforward and at the end a senior officer interviewed me. He congratulated me on gaining the highest score that the career office had achieved to date, then left me to study a folder that detailed all the opportunities open to me in the Army. I quickly rejected the options of vehicle mechanic, cartographer, signals engineer, etc. I already knew what I wanted – to join the Paras. The careers officer was disappointed; he clearly was not a fan of the Parachute Regiment.

At this point he showed me a folder that detailed the role of the Intelligence Corps; this was obviously his passion. He explained that my exam score was good enough for entry into the training system, and he could arrange an interview with the Intelligence Corps's own careers officer. I turned down the offer. The Paras were still my number one choice. I was given a sum of money, about twenty pounds, and a rail warrant to travel to Manchester Army Careers Offices, where myself, and about ten others, swore an oath of allegiance to our sovereign, Queen Elizabeth II.

I lasted all of ten weeks in the Paras. I failed no courses and found the physical side a challenge, but not outside my capabilities, but it was just not what I expected. My section commander noticed the decline in my enthusiasm and conveyed this to my platoon commander, Lt Adams. To cut a long story short, he recommended that I make contact with an Intelligence Corps careers warrant officer. At Templar Barracks in Ashford in Kent I underwent two interviews, a language test and a psychiatric test, and was told I was suitable. Some weeks later I joined 85 Squadron.

The social life at Templar Barracks was hectic, and, given my gregarious nature, it was not long before my coursework began to suffer. Having failed three consecutive weekly tests, myself and my best friend Kev were backsquadded to Squad 90. By the way, the test involved being able to draw a complete motor-ised regiment of the Russian Army, everything from the number of men, the number of vehicles and the constituent parts belonging to the nuclear, biological and chemical unit!

Second time around, we were prepared for the exams. Kev and I had built up an extensive knowledge of how the training wing worked. We had noted that the keys to the classified storage area were kept in a locked, secure, upright locker; the key to this locker was in turn stored in the Chief Clerk's desk. Each week, usually on the Wednesday night before a Friday exam, we broke into the offices, dismantled the top to the desk, removed the keys to the locker, opened the locker, removed the keys to the classified waste area and stole the carbon copy which had been used to print the exam papers. *Voilà!* From being bottom of the class in Squad 85, suddenly we were perfectly placed in Squad 90 – not at the front of the class, because that would have been obvious, but just behind. I suppose we played the game by intelligence rules; we used our initiative and in many ways that experience taught us many valuable lessons. At the end of training, I passed all my exams and was now a lance corporal in the Intelligence Corps.

My first posting was to Northern Ireland in 1981 to a small unit dealing with the input of agent material directly onto the computer system. I then moved to Headquarters Northern Ireland (HQNI), where I worked for 121 Intelligence Section. This section supported the general staff and required a level one access – the highest level of security clearance. In 1982 I applied for 'special duties', in other words, to become part of FRU. For anyone involved in the intelligence world, FRU was the cutting edge; if you worked for the FRU you were at the 'coalface'. After completing my FRU training, I was sent to FRU North, based in Derry. In late 1984 my father became seriously ill with a heart condition and I was posted to a security location close to my hometown in England, to be near him. I was also promoted to the rank of sergeant.

Around that time, Willie Carlin, a former Sinn Féin treasurer and Frank Hegarty, a former quartermaster of the Provisional IRA, were exposed as FRU agents. Because I had a working knowledge of both parties, I was seconded to L Branch of Repton Manor, in Templar Barracks, which was the Special Intelligence Wing (SIW) unit given responsibility for dealing with resettlement of agents. After this I was posted to York Security Section and then seconded for six months to Belize in Central America, where we were keeping a close eye upon the Nicaraguan situation and the flourishing drug trade.

I returned to England in 1987 and went to Templar Barracks for another FRU course, which was required before I could be sent back to Northern Ireland. I was then posted to FRU West, in Enniskillen. During my tour of FRU West, I met a young lady who was to become very important to me. She was a native of the Republic, working and living in Northern Ireland. I had carried out background checks on her, using the computer and local police, and discovered that she had family links with known or wanted republicans. Being a person who works from instinct and my own wits, I was reasonably certain that she herself posed no security risk, either to the unit or to me. We formed a relationship and she became well known to the other members of the local FRU.

About twelve months later, in late 1990, I applied for, and secured, a plum post at the Ministry Of Defence in Whitehall,

London, whereupon I left FRU. On my posting to the MOD I informed the vetting authorities, as I was required to do, that I was living with this lady and that I intended to marry her. They carried out their own checks and found the same family links to republicans as I had some twelve months earlier. My vetting was due for a five-year review, and it was made clear that while my vetting outside Northern Ireland would not be affected, any future posting back to Northern Ireland would not be in a sensitive role. That posed big problems for me; the MOD job would be a two-year stint, after which I would be put back into the 'mixer' with everyone else, and could be posted to an unrewarding job in Germany or elsewhere. My expertise was in Northern Ireland; I enjoyed the work and the people, and it was where I felt I could best advance my career. So, I had to make a choice – give up my girlfriend or give up the Intelligence Corps.

I chose my girlfriend, who is now my wife. I applied for, and after some difficulty was granted, the right to buy my way out of the Army, leaving for good in 1991 with an exemplary record. The Army and myself parted on good terms. It had been a good employer. But, in the light of what follows, I would issue one caution to any soldier of the Intelligence Corps: evil only requires decent people to turn a blind eye for a moment to flourish.

✳ ✳ ✳

The Force Research Unit (FRU) was a British Army Intelligence Corps unit working in Northern Ireland, recruiting, developing and controlling the Army's 'human intelligence' assets in Britain's secret war on the IRA. Its motto was 'Fishers of Men'. It was sponsored and funded by the Director of

Special Forces (DSF). The FRU operated from 1980 up until the early 1990s when its name was changed to the Joint Services Group (JSG). The name change was necessary for political and symbolic reasons after the arrest of Brian Nelson by the Stevens Inquiry, the long-running investigation into collusion between British security forces and paramilitary organisations in Northern Ireland, being led by Metropolitan Police Commissioner, Sir John Stevens, and the subsequent conviction of the former agent. That said, neither the role nor operating methods of the FRU were affected either by the name change or by the exposure of its methods during the short court case. There had, of course, been similar military organisations involved in intelligence-gathering in Northern Ireland prior to the FRU, for example, the Mobile Reconnaissance Force (MRF). However, a lack of control and problems of centralisation meant that these units were deemed by both politicians and the military to be largely inefficient. They did not achieve significant successes in either preventing or frustrating the operations of terrorist organisations.

The Intelligence Corps performs intelligence-gathering operations in every operational theatre in which the British Army works. It also gathers intelligence in places where there are no troops on the ground. In the case of the Troubles, that means the Republic of Ireland. The operating methods of the FRU are not unique – the principles of handling human intelligence are the same, whether it be in Belize, Kosovo, Baghdad or on the streets of Derry.

The Army's Intelligence Corps has, from the early 1990s, been based in Templar Barracks, Ashford, Kent. The FRU was based at Repton Manor, within Templar Barracks. 'The manor', as it was known to operators and students alike, was a medieval building, in many ways unsuitable for conventional military training. However, the FRU is not a conventional unit, and the manor – tucked away in a far corner of the large military establishment – was an ideal location for the purpose of training the Army's elite band of human intelligence. It became a sort of home-from-home to most handlers.

During my FRU training it became obvious that there was no textbook in existence that could show you the right way to cope with the many different situations and scenarios that you would be involved in as a handler. Experience was a major asset and every detachment had a fair share of the 'old guard' – operators with, ideally, more than two FRU tours of service – alongside new recruits. This made for a good blend of youthful enthusiasm and the reliability of more experienced operators.

The place had a certain aura about it. In a small garden area to the front of the manor was a large oak tree that had reputedly been used to hang 'witches' during the Cromwellian era. There were many stories of ghosts and strange sightings, and there were very few who would volunteer to be the last person out of the building in the evening. Having turned the lights out on the upper floors, it seemed an eternity before you arrived at the large and imposing front door.

The FRU was manned by officers of the Intelligence Corps and by soldiers from all the British services. The operators, or handlers, were themselves recruited from all three services – Royal Navy, Army and Royal Air Force and included both men and women. Approximately forty percent of FRU handlers were drawn from sources other than the services' intelligence corps. Initially a prospective handler would apply for 'special duties'. The applicant would be invited to a preliminary interview where his or her suitability would be assessed. Should the interviewer recommend the applicant, he or she would be allocated a place on a three-day pre-selection course, designed to show the service person what 'special duties' work entailed, and giving either the applicant or the FRU the opportunity to halt the process at that stage.

The pre-selection course would involve many tasks. For instance, the prospective FRU student would be asked to go to a designated public house and engage a total stranger (of the same sex) in conversation. During this conversation, the student would attempt to extract from the unsuspecting member of the public various pieces of information, for example: name, address, date of birth, family details, home telephone number, job, place of work, hobbies, vehicle type, etc. The information extracted could be authenticated by the directing staff using local knowledge, electoral registers and, of course, the local police. This exercise was a reliable gauge of whether the prospective student could strike up a 'cold relationship' with a member of the public and gather intelligence, much as a handler would when targeting a prospective agent. The failure rate on the pre-selection course was approximately four out of five.

Successful applicants would next be offered a place on the full eight-week FRU course at the manor. Servicemen from the normal 'green' Army would now be joined by other students, such as myself, from the Intelligence Corps. An average course would comprise ten students, of whom approximately three to five would successfully complete the course.

The manor was home to many courses, on subjects such as interrogation, covert method of entry, aerial reconnaissance (photo recognition), etc. The building was an absolute labyrinth of many small rooms, some hardly bigger than a large toilet. Some of these rooms were turned into 'interrogation' rooms; they were soundproofed and programmed with 'white noise', a low emission noise made up of a combination of all the different frequencies of sound, which effectively masked other noises, causing sensory deprivation – useful for isolating and disorientating the person being interrogated. The whole complex, from photographic rooms and classrooms to observation rooms, was fitted with CCTV, fed to a staff control room. The cameras were invaluable to the directing staff – every action and every word could be analysed, helping to determine a student's suitability for FRU work. It was a bit like the modern-day 'Big Brother' television programme.

Possibly the most important facility in the complex, a facility essential to any military establishment, was located in a very old, long barn adjacent to the main house. This building was known to operators by the not too subtle cover name 'the Barn'. It was, of course, the bar, a vital cog in the Intelligence Corps social scene. In military and police circles the bar is invaluable. It is a place of business, where failures of the day can be discussed and relationships and personalities can be developed or analysed. On the flip side, I know of many students who earned a ticket back to their home unit because of their failure to understand that even in the bar, pitched into the middle of a riotous piss-up, you were still under the microscope of the directing staff, still being evaluated for suitability for the FRU. Perhaps this explains why the failure rate for students was so high. Other than Intelligence Corps applicants, a student was extremely unlikely to be granted two bites at the cherry. Failure meant that a student was given a Returned to Unit (RTU) notification and a free train ticket; normally they were escorted off the manor grounds within minutes of being notified of the RTU instruction.

✳ ✳ ✳

The FRU was established with unique terms of reference – unlike other intelligence units operating in Northern Ireland, such as the Special Air Service (SAS) or 14th Intelligence Company, it did not have an RUC officer commanding operations. Essentially, the authorities wanted to have an independent 'eyes and ears' coverage of the changing situation in Northern Ireland. A member of MI5 who was based in the FRU operations office (HQNI), saw all the material generated by FRU and channelled it upwards. Because of the way it was structured, the Force Research Unit had unprecedented room for flexibility within the field of operations. And make no mistake about it, that field of operations extended to every county in Ireland, not just the six which make up Northern Ireland.

A major difficulty in Northern Ireland for all sections of the security forces has been the multi-agency approach. The old saying about too many cooks spoiling the broth was never truer than it was in Northern Ireland. The relationship between the FRU and RUC Special Branch was frosty. The Army has far more experience at operating in a counter-terrorist role than either MI5 or RUC Special Branch. Nevertheless, the RUC fought hard over a long number of years to restrict the Army's involvement in intelligence-gathering, or at least to operations the RUC did not control and direct.

People might imagine that the intelligence community worked like a piece of well-oiled German engineering, but this perception is entirely wrong. The internal squabbles could be childish at times. Without doubt they led to inefficiency, and sometimes to loss of life. One of the primary principles of intelligence-gathering is central coordination, but this principle was totally overlooked. The RUC had police primacy in Northern Ireland, and RUC Special Branch was the primary intelligence unit in the six counties. The British Army brought three undercover units to the party – 22 Squadron SAS, which undertook 'executive actions', 14 Company, specialising in covert surveillance and FRU. The security services (MI5) brought their agent-handling and electronic technical expertise to the table. These units, plus Special Branch, were commonly described as the intelligence community.

The problem that the community suffered was a basic one – little or no coordination, due mainly to the intense distrust between the various agencies. Imagine a fishing competition, with three teams each trying to land the biggest catch of fish possible. There is a significant prize for the team that wins, but if the three teams between them can reach a high enough aggregate target, they will qualify for a major international competition where the glory, and the prize-money, will be considerably larger. The reservoir chosen for the competition is large but not well stocked with the prime fish. The three teams each have their own ideas of the best methods to land the largest catch. Instead of working together, they get caught up in rivalry and members of each team attempt to deliberately foul the fishing lines of their competitors to try to deny them a catch, completely losing sight of the ultimate prize – the aggregate catch.

For example, I know from conversations with Stakeknife's

handlers that RUC Special Branch made a number of hostile attempts to lure him away from the Army to the Branch. He was threatened by the Branch, told that if he did not go to work for them his details would be leaked to the IRA and his fate would be certain death. Wisely, and to the relief of his Army handlers, Stakeknife refused their kind offer of alternative employment.

As handlers in Northern Ireland we knew that our lives and the lives of our agents depended solely on our training and our ability to infiltrate the enemy. We used lots of different methods to infiltrate the enemy, and lots of different types of agents. Our political masters described the Troubles as a conflict. It wasn't. It was a war, albeit an unconventional one, that crossed international boundaries.

Our motivation and the motivation of our agents were often different, but they all served a similar purpose. When I was first posted to Northern Ireland I was told that there was only one enemy – the Provisional IRA. With hindsight I realise that every single resource was pitched against republicans. There was absolutely no direction from the top to take on loyalism. Although politicians have claimed that the FRU was directed at both loyalist and republican paramilitaries, this is simply untrue. It did not recruit loyalists. The truth is that the FRU was prevented by RUC Special Branch from infiltrating loyalist murder gangs. The exception to FRU's policy of not recruiting loyalists was Brian Nelson. But then, Nelson, although a loyalist, was also a former British Army soldier and thus outside the normal terms of reference. And while Nelson did infiltrate loyalist paramilitary groups, his information was used by FRU not against loyalists but against republicans and ordinary Catholics.

It is my belief that there is a place and a role in all decent democratic societies for an intelligence agency that is working towards acceptable goals. To that end I would defend ninety-nine percent of all FRU operations during the periods in which I was involved. The one percent of operations that, in my opinion, cannot be defended should, I believe, be brought out into the open and the lessons learnt from these operations should be incorporated into the terms of reference for the entire intelligence community. We must admit our mistakes, go some way to make good those mistakes, and learn from them so we do not repeat them.

I do not regret my role in the war. I do regret, however, that certain lines, certain moral boundaries were stepped over too many times and innocent people died. There are many people who have been 'touched' by the activities of the FRU. In some cases this 'touch' resulted in people being killed or injured; others suffered loss or damage to property without ever being aware that they had been the victims of a state-employed agent. Innocent people were killed, having been labelled informers, and their families had to live with both the grief and the stigma. In some of these cases the IRA has recently offered apologies, acknowledging that the victims were not informers.

I believe that the families of all the innocent people 'touched' by the FRU have a right to know what happened to their loved ones. That is one motivation in writing this book.

And I have another motivation – support for the peace process and the Good Friday Agreement. It is my sincere hope that it will be saved, but in order to move on we must all deal with our past.

Chapter 2

Recruiting and Running an Agent

Ingram

British military intelligence has many years of experience at running networks of agents in hostile conditions. It has a large pool of highly trained handlers available for duty anywhere in the world. In Northern Ireland they operated under the Force Research Unit.

The running of an undercover network is a complex operation. In fact, it takes an extraordinary amount of resources to develop and maintain even one agent. A productive agent is an agent who is happy, both at home and work, so a lot of time and effort is taken up with welfare issues. A good handler will act almost as a social worker, reassuring the agent that he has his best interests, and the interests of his family, at heart.

Having worked with many agents in my career, I discovered one predominant common denominator in their personalities: their willingness and ability to lie. And when I mean lie, I mean the ability to lie to their families in most cases, certainly to their friends and, where appropriate, comrades, and on occasions, of course, to their handlers – us.

Making contact

The first step in recruiting an agent was to establish a point of contact. This involved some research on the potential recruit. In order to get alongside his target, the handler would gather information to build up a picture of the target's movements, including routes habitually taken, and dates and timings of all activities.

Before approaching a target, the handler would also assess their degree of value to the FRU, for instance, if they had access to a subversive organisation. The ideal recruit would, of course, have direct access to paramilitaries. However, it could also be productive to recruit persons who might have good indirect access, perhaps a 'courier' or a taxi driver who drove suspects around on their business. An advantage of 'active' volunteers was that they were surveillance-aware and more cautious and watchful than those on the periphery.

In Northern Ireland, recruiting at a target's place of work was unusual, because the majority of targets were unemployed – not by choice, but because unemployment in republican areas is historically high.

A target's home was not usually considered a good point of contact and was seldom used, because the target feels more secure in his own environment and is less likely to be receptive to an approach. Places of leisure were ideal. For example, if the target was a fisherman or a keen swimmer; these hobbies allowed the target to be isolated and the process of 'pitching' undertaken in an environment controlled by the handler.

It is possible to artificially create a point of contact – for instance, a target could be made to believe that he had won a prize in a draw and be invited to a local hotel to collect it. Other opportunities arose where a target was selling his house or car. A viewing would be arranged by the handler, posing as a prospective purchaser. He would make a very attractive offer for the property; say £120,000 for a house valued at £85,000. If the target went along with the approach, even though there was obviously more to this than a genuine transaction, then he was hooked. He would be paid the asking price for the house, and given the extra £35,000 as a 'sweetener'. This method had a high success rate and was a relatively easy and safe way of getting alongside the target.

This first step of the recruiting operation took a great deal of planning and was by far the most time consuming. But if it worked out, then it was worth it.

Establishing motivation

Once a point of contact had been set up, motivational factors had to be examined. Why would someone become an agent? What made them open to an approach in the first place? My experience and that of other handlers I worked with would suggest that there are as many motivating factors as there are agents. A handler would carry out extensive research to determine the motivation of a potential agent, as this could make the difference between acquiring a valuable agent and one who could be unreliable, or worse, still, 'turned' by the other side.

Revenge was probably the best motivation for any potential recruit. An individual might have received a beating by members of a subversive organisation, such as the provisional IRA. Immediately after such a beating the target might be receptive to an approach, motivated purely by revenge. It must be remembered that from small acorns oak trees grow – a youth given a beating by the IRA for some possibly minor 'infringement' could later turn into a major headache for the organisation as a result.

Another common reason for targets to turn was when a particular event caused them to adopt an anti-violence stance. After every outrage in Northern Ireland there was a high degree of revulsion in the local community. Within hours after a major incident, for example the Memorial Day massacre at Enniskillen or the Omagh bombing, there would be a concerted effort by the FRU and other agencies to tap into this rich vein of outrage and condemnation. In the Shankill Road bombing on 23 October 1993, nine Protestant civilians and one IRA man died in the attack on Frizzel's fish shop. The IRA's intended target was the UDA inner council, who had offices above the shop, but the operation went completely wrong. The Shankill bombing marked the beginning of a dark week in the history of the Troubles in Northern Ireland. Six Catholics were killed in loyalist attacks in the next six days, and seven days after the fish-shop bombing, the Ulster Freedom Fighters (UFF) burst into the Rising Sun bar in Greysteel, County Derry and murdered seven more people. In such times, all State agencies involved in intelligence-gathering would try to capitalise on the feelings stirred up by the atrocities by 'turning' informants and making pitches to those they believed could help the security forces bring an end to such outrages. But handlers had to move quickly on these occasions. In the volatile nature of the Northern Ireland conflict, yesterday's outrage and revulsion could very quickly fade, to be replaced once again by sympathy toward the paramilitary.

Recruitment amongst anti-violence splinter groups like the Official IRA was also important, though most informers among their ranks worked for Special Branch rather than FRU.

Many agents have worked for the security forces for one reason and one reason alone – good, old-fashioned greed. In the course of research, a target might be identified as having financial difficulties – a free-spending wife or an accident in a third-party-only insured vehicle were common starting points for an approach. It is amazing what can happen when a briefcase containing Stg£20,000 in crisp, clean £50 notes is placed under the nose of a target. Even the most hardened paramilitaries have succumbed to the lure of money and the FRU, unlike the RUC, had access to limitless supplies of cash, being supplied by the Director of Special Forces. Each FRU detachment had a safe that contained a float, usually around the £10,000 mark; this money was used to pay agents and also any expenses incurred on a daily basis. If bigger amounts were required, they could readily be obtained from FRU HQ. Large sums would be offered to entice a prospective agent; I myself was involved in two operations where the amount on offer was £20,000. Having said that, I have never seen such an amount actually paid over; it was usually a teaser, the agent would have to work very hard to achieve that sort of remuneration.

There were other motivational factors. In some border areas there were recruits from a revolutionary or left wing background who saw the IRA's targeting of Protestant farmers, many of whom were part-time members of the police or UDR, as sectarian. A number of old republicans did not, or would not, subscribe to what they saw as ethnic cleansing against the Protestant communities in border regions.

Blackmail is a method used by police forces the world over to get cooperation from unwilling targets. In my experience, however, the Army has never utilised this as a tool in the recruitment of agents. Blackmail is a difficult motivation to control and it usually ends in an abrupt and unpredictable manner. As handlers, we tried not to use it, because you always have to remember that an agent who you are blackmailing is not on your side. The RUC used blackmail extensively and many of its agents ended up dead.

Unlike other agencies, the Army would also not use threats or non-monetary 'sweeteners', for example, an amnesty from drink driving, burglary or drug pushing charges. This sort of motivation in an agent is also difficult to control. The RUC specialised in these tactics and history has shown that RUC agents had a distinctly shorter shelf life as a result.

And then, of course, there were people who became agents for the 'buzz'. It gave them a status, a sense of being important. They enjoyed the secrecy, the sense of danger and the feeling of belonging to the intelligence 'family'. Money was not usually a prime factor for these agents, but they needed a lot of validation, of being told what a good job they were doing.

'Walk-in' agents

Many of the best agents who worked for the Army just walked in off the street and volunteered their services. Unbelievable as it may seem, Stakeknife was an example of such an agent; his motives are dealt with later in the book.

The first approach from a volunteer agent would be dealt with by an Army unit that was on station, carrying out normal *roulement* duties (serving on rotation for short periods). The individual would initially meet the unit intelligence officer (IO), who would confirm personal details and make an evaluation of the information on offer. The IO would certainly have been briefed in outline on the FRU's role prior to his tour of duty, and he would be able to assess the FRU's possible interest in the potential of this person. Should he be deemed of sufficient interest to the FRU, he would be taken under their wing, on his way to becoming an active agent.

There were major security concerns when dealing with a 'walk-in', both for the FRU and the person concerned. The FRU was risking entrapment by someone who was not 'kosher', and the 'walk-in' was risking exposure, and possibly his life, if there was any security leak that betrayed him to his own side. Persons other than FRU members would know the identity of the new and potentially valuable asset. The IO and any other soldiers who were aware of his identity would be given advice on how to conduct themselves. If the agent was of significant importance, those with knowledge might well be withdrawn from the theatre as a security measure and redeployed far away, perhaps in Germany. The risk factor for the handler and his cover team was very high during contact in the early days of such a relationship, because the possibility of the 'walk-in' being a double agent was considerable. Subversive organisations have in the past used this method to set up handlers, so the team involved would need to be extra vigilant. However, to place some perspective on this risk, some of the best agents the Army worked with have been volunteers or 'walk-ins', especially when their motivation was based on revenge.

Closing the deal

Before an agent could be 'handled', he or she first had to be recruited. Not all FRU handlers were keen on undertaking recruitment because this was often the hardest part of the job. Some were more skilled than others at 'closing the deal' and getting the customer to sign up. A handler could have carried out exhaustive research and have successfully identified many of the attributes that would make a good agent, but if he could not make a successful 'pitch' when he was in position, then all the time and effort would have been wasted. Even for experienced handlers, it was all too easy to fumble and lose momentum, and thus simply fail to close the deal.

Real-life case histories
The one that got away

During the late 1980s there was a dramatic escalation of violence along the Donegal border, particularly in the Ballyshannon/Bundoran area. The IRA unit that had been operating in the area for some time was extremely ruthless – even within the republican movement they had a reputation for being unpredictable. A leading member had been seriously injured when an ambush of security forces in which he was involved, was compromised. The operation involved SAS members. In the ensuing firefight one SAS man and one paramilitary died.

The Ballyshannon/Bundoran IRA unit included many experienced but elderly volunteers. The upsurge in violence during the late 1980s coincided with a number of more youthful members joining the movement. I was working at the time as a handler attached to FRU West at St Angelo (Enniskillen), an area where the FRU had little high-grade material. RUC intelligence had reported the presence of a potential agent, a young man who lived in close proximity to the border on the northern side. His family, although not directly involved in the Troubles, were sympathetic to the Provisionals and distinctly cold towards any security force patrols who might call for a cup of tea. This target had been actively involved in a number of murders over a short period, including those of Gillian Johnston, a Protestant who was killed when the IRA targeted a family member who they believed was in the UDR, and former RUC Constable Harold Keys, whose girlfriend was from the Republic.

A point of contact was difficult to establish, because the target was unemployed but did not claim benefit in the North. He used the family home only occasionally – not out of fear of any loyalist or security force attention, but merely because his work within the republican movement involved him renting accommodation in the Ballyshannon area, in the Irish Republic.

Over a period of months I visited the target's family home on a number of occasions, hoping to meet him. Initially I was disguised as part of a normal 'green' Army patrol. Subsequently, I organised a patrol made up of other FRU members. The intention was to get alongside the target, assess the likelihood of a successful approach and gauge his probable reaction to a sizeable briefcase of money being placed under his nose. When we eventually met him, we quickly concluded that the target was cocky and confident and that he felt he had nothing to fear from the Army. The impression I gained was of an individual who was unlikely to be susceptible to a normal 'straight pitch'. In a number of encounters, the target was left in no doubt that he was being examined by military intelligence. Initially he was intrigued by the attention. I suggested a game of pool one evening in a 'safe' pub, and he quickly told me to 'fuck off' – not in a violent tone, merely with an incredulity at the prospect of playing pool with an intelligence handler.

Our FRU unit had an existing and fairly reliable agent in Ballyshannon who had been tasked to monitor this individual and report his movements to his handler. This agent was not informed that the individual he was monitoring was a potential target of the FRU. Our agent easily identified the flat that the target was using. The flat was ideally located for surveillance purposes, above a row of shops in Ballyshannon town centre. It was decided to carry out a reconnaissance of the area to decide whether it presented a reasonably safe environment in which to 'bump' the target. This could mean anything from literally bumping into him on the street, to arranging to back into his car, causing minor damage, but resulting in insurance and other details being exchanged.

Before any incursions were undertaken into the Republic of Ireland permission was required from the Commander Land Forces (CLF). The Commanding Officer FRU secured the permission and, along with a fellow handler, I carried out a full reconnaissance of the routes in and out of Ballyshannon without sighting the target.

The door of his flat was slightly recessed, allowing a certain amount of cover, and it was decided by the team that the best way of gaining the attention of the target was to stand in the doorway. The intention was not to engage him in conversation, but merely to make a 'brush contact' – once he had recognised me, I would simply walk casually away. The surveillance team was responsible for both my security and the approach to the target's flat. If the target was accompanied, the operation would be aborted.

The operation went ahead without any problems. The target nearly choked on his fish supper when he saw me, who he knew to be a British soldier, standing in his doorway. Without saying a word, he ran for his life, dropping his supper in his haste to escape. As can happen in these cases, the target was not sighted in the North for a long time after that. Our existing agent in Ballyshannon reported that the target moved flats immediately after the 'brush contact'.

Over the next twelve months a number of attempts were made to get alongside the target, but all were unsuccessful. The success rate in this type of operation is approximately one in every twenty attempts, and this wasn't one of them. We never managed to recruit this young man; today he is a leading dissident republican.

Patience is an absolute prerequisite for a handler.

Brian – a success story

Brian was a hard nut to crack. He was a top player in the Provisional IRA in the west of Northern Ireland, and it was my job to get him to work for the British Army. Brian had an intense dislike of the RUC and the UDR, but in casual contacts with Army patrols he had shown a certain respect for the Army and an understanding of the difficulties we worked under.

Handlers sometimes posed as civilians when dealing with targets, and at other times in their military capacity. It was decided that Brian was so high up in the local IRA unit that the safest option was a military front-up. Exposing a handler's civilian front at this level was deemed too dangerous. I duly donned the uniform of the British regiment on tour in the area at the time and targeted the potential recruit with a planned vehicle checkpoint.

Paramilitaries are taught never to talk to police interrogators while in custody. The best IRA operatives refused to engage in any conversation at checkpoints, as opening up in any way to the enemy was deemed too dangerous. I decided to play my cards – literally – on Brian. I was the lead on a Vehicle Check Point (VCP) when Brian's car was stopped. As Brian handed over his driving licence, I asked him how he was, but there was no reply. I told the top Provisional that he would have to wait for a check to be carried out on the licence. Then I asked another soldier to fetch a small box from the back of the British Army Land Rover. It was a box of card questions from the game of Trivial Pursuit. I gave the astonished Brian a choice: answer the question correctly or be held for up to four hours under the Emergency Provisions Act. Brian burst out laughing. A conversation began – the first step in building up a rapport with the target. My ploy had been simple, but effective. I did this again over a period of months, and we finally progressed to having a game of pool together. Brian eventually began to work for the FRU, partly, I think, because of his hatred of the RUC/UDR and partly because he had become sickened by extreme violence and felt he was helping towards preventing further loss of life.

***

Protecting your agent

It was generally held in the intelligence community that the RUC were not professional 'intelligencers', as we called ourselves. Without the correct training and approach, they lost good potential assets and failed to extract the maximum intelligence value from their agents. RUC Special Branch received no formal intelligence training and was expected to 'run' assets with no experience other than that gained in stumbling from one botched job to another. An excellent insight into this lack of professionalism can be read in the book *Phoenix*, which was researched by Superintendent Ian Phoenix, with the intention of publishing it when he retired. He was killed in the Chinook helicopter crash on the Mull of Kintyre in 1994, and the book subsequently appeared under the name of his wife and Jack Holland.

Ian Phoenix was a Tasking and Coordinating Group (TCG) officer, responsible for administering tactical intelligence gathered by agencies operating in Northern Ireland. The book chronicles the petty jealousies and back-stabbing that were common, and gives details of one instance where operators refused to carry out a lawful command. A team of undercover policemen who were trained for surveillance duties, and took extra payment for this work, decided that they did not fancy spending the evening in a cold, wet and hostile environment, so they went home. This situation would never, ever, have occurred in a well-disciplined and motivated military unit. Those police officers were not punished for their insubordination and were allowed to carry out operations the following day as if nothing untoward had happened. Being an ex-Para, Phoenix found this behaviour completely unacceptable although there was little he could do except fight for the option to use military assets rather than RUC assets in hostile environments. As I have said, Special Branch or its E4 unit were not, and are not, professional intelligencers and it is folly to believe that people did not die as a result of this policy. It is an indisputable fact that the Army has managed to keep agent losses to a minimum over the years, while the RUC's record, in contrast, is littered with obituaries and hard-luck stories. I can think of no finer illustration of this point than the controversial shooting of Seamus Grew (INLA) and Roddy Carroll (INLA) in December 1982.

On the evening of 12 December 1982, a covert RUC unit, who operated on both sides of the border, had set up an ambush for Dominic McGlinchey (an INLA man on the run), based on intelligence supplied to them by an informer. The agent had told them that McGlinchey – at that time the most wanted man in Ireland – would be travelling to a specified area in a motor vehicle also occupied by Grew and Carroll. The trap was sprung and Grew and Carroll were both shot. But the main target of the ambush, McGlinchey, had left the vehicle some minutes before the ambush and escaped. The Stalker Inquiry carried out an investigation into this incident and at least two other contentious incidents in the mid-eighties to establish or refute the accusations of a 'shoot to kill' policy within the RUC. For reasons of 'national security', Stalker was not told the identity of the RUC informer, but in May 1983, five months after the ambush, Eric Dale (INLA) was interrogated and executed by Mary McGlinchey and her husband Dominic. By a process of elimination and having observed police actions, they had successfully deduced Dale's true allegiance. Both Dominic and Mary McGlinchey interrogated Dale; indeed Mary McGlinchey sat Dale on the electric rings/plates of a cooker hob. His body was recovered near Killeen in south Armagh by Sinn Féin. It is my belief, based on an RUC B2* source, that Dale's death was a direct result of the bungled operation mounted by the RUC on 12 December 1982, which also led to the deaths of Grew and Carroll. The way the RUC acted upon the information supplied by Dale pointed directly at him as the informant. With a degree of professionalism and imagination an alternative to this type of operation would have been far more conducive to both the agent and the RUC.

This episode highlights poor handling and case management techniques by the RUC, an area where its training continues to leave a lot to be desired. *Phoenix* also illustrates the lack of strategy and planning that occurred in the case of agent Carol – Marty McGartland, author of *Fifty Dead Men Walking* – who was exposed to the 'Ra' by poor handling technique, which demonstrated a total disregard for the safety of a fellow human being. I would recommend reading both books and looking at the conflicting evidence surrounding the abduction and subsequent imprisonment of the agent by the Provisional IRA (PIRA).

*Grading of source information

A system of grading is used in the intelligence community when circulating information. The grading runs from A to F and from 1 to 6. A handler will mark the appropriate grading on information supplied to him by an agent or other source, so that the person reading the information can evaluate its reliability and intelligence significance. An A1 source is a fact, eg a known event. A B2 is the best category of source information. B indicates that the reliability of the source is good and 2 indicates that the probability of information is high, or that there is good collateral evidence to back it up. This B grading would only be attributed to an agent who had demonstrated his reliability over a period of time. Where a piece of information was graded F6, it would mean that the source, F, could not be relied upon, either because of inexperience or because he had a track record of unreliability. The 6 would indicate to the reader that there was no collateral for the report and that there was a low probability of the information being true, or that it was not possible to accurately assess it.

Chapter 3

Human Intelligence

Ingram

Ever since man began to walk he has recognised the benefits of having advance knowledge of what his adversary is planning. It allows countermeasures to be put in place, helping to neutralise a threat and ideally enabling the tables to be turned from defence to offence.

In our advanced technological age there are a bewildering number of artificial ways in which knowledge can be obtained, so why is there still such widespread use of people as intelligence gatherers? There are both advantages and disadvantages to working with human sources as opposed to other sources of intelligence. The advantage of a human source over, say, a fixed electronic listening device is the ability to task, or direct, an agent to seek the answer to a question, to track down information. An electronic device also has limitations of distance, fuel life, and so on. On the other hand, dealing with human beings can be fraught with problems; agents, like everyone else, have personal difficulties – matrimonial and financial complications, for example. A bug cannot lie, unless it has been compromised, whereas agents are notorious and accomplished liars. To illustrate some of the difficulties associated with agent handling, a number of real cases are outlined below. These brief glimpses into the lives of agents will demonstrate both sides of the coin.

Brenda

One case study which illustrates the benefits of working with a 'willing' agent is that of a lady we knew in the FRU as Busty Brenda, (now deceased, of natural causes). From a rural area of Fermanagh, Brenda was in her thirties, single and a Catholic. A farmer by trade, she was blessed with decency and solid values. The story of her recruitment is not unusual. It started one morning when I was nosing around the local UDR intelligence cell. They had a file entitled 'Tea Stops' and in this file were names and addresses of houses and farms where uniformed soldiers were welcome. This information would have been built up over a period of time by Army patrols, who would call to houses in fairly 'safe areas' on their route and gauge the reaction of the occupants. If, after a number of visits, the patrol was offered a cup of tea, the householders might be viewed as potential targets for FRU work. Details were also kept for another reason – the UDR was concerned to keep a watchful eye on any location or individual who was prepared to offer tea or protection from the elements. Rightly, they feared a set-up.

A number of patrols had reported the use of a particular house, and they also recorded the details of the lady owner. I surreptitiously copied down the details. Then I made plans for an FRU uniformed patrol, in which I was included, to visit the house to assess the target's potential as a possible agent, and over a period of weeks a number of visits were made. On all these visits I was accompanied by a young collator, who I will call Mike and who, I am sure, went on acquit himself well after I left the FRU.

Unfortunately, the target was always accompanied by a friend who did not fit my criteria as a possible agent. Mike was tasked to befriend the friend, allowing me to isolate and develop a relationship with the target. It was soon clear that the potential agent had no direct access to any republican organisation, although she socialised and mixed in the right company. Without her friend knowing, Brenda accepted my offer to 'work' and from that moment on she was a dedicated and loyal agent. Her motivation was a mixture of friendship towards me, and revulsion at violence.

Initially, as a new agent on the periphery of the republican community, Brenda was given basic jobs – visiting pubs and making herself known to the right people. Over a period of months I suggested she join Sinn Féin, making herself available to help in the local area – nothing sinister, but useful when building an image and confidence. She relished her role as an agent, always carrying out her tasks willingly and with a smile. There was a certain chemistry which evolved over the years between myself and Brenda; nothing sexual, but we hit it off, as they say. This friendship was encouraged as part of Brenda's motivation in continuing to work for the FRU.

When Brenda was recruited, she made no request for money. However, I insisted on payment, knowing well that money leads to a degree of dependence. Still, Brenda received only a small financial retainer for her services, although we, of course, financed any expenses incurred in entertaining or socialising in connection with her FRU work. Brenda developed into an excellent 'eyes and ears' agent. I understand that she continued to progress after I left the FRU, although sadly she succumbed to cancer and later died. But she was a great lady who had provided valuable information on both sides of the border, and that information saved lives. Even though she is dead, it would be reckless to give details on whose lives she saved, or where, but one of Brenda's most successful operations involved a 'close liaison' – in layman's terms, sleeping with the enemy.

One prominent married local IRA man was a favourite target for this lady. Let's call him John. Brenda's instructions were clear: gain John's confidence by using her feminine charms. Knowing when the target would be away from home allowed specialist intelligence agencies to gain access to the man's home and plant listening devices, without worry that the team would be compromised by the Provo. Once Brenda herself had inveigled her way into his house, John began to talk, as is common when people are in the security of their own homes.

Over and over again in the Troubles, information revealed in this way exposed locations of arms and ammunition and leaked details of impending operations. The intelligence services would then set up surveillance on the operation or steal the compromised arms caches, which led to the paramilitaries involved being compromised to their own organisations. Often the IRA's internal security department would hunt for an informer who didn't exist, when electronic surveillance was the key tool. An example of this is the killings of several IRA members at Loughgall police station in May 1987. In a private house, which, unknown to them, was bugged, the IRA had openly discussed their plans for the attack on the station.

The information gained from Brenda's contact with John proved invaluable over a considerable period of time.

✳ ✳ ✳

Seamus

Another case that illustrates the pros and cons of human intelligence is that of an agent we will call Seamus, a resident of the Republic, living on the Fermanagh/Cavan border. At various times in his long career, Seamus was co-handled by both FRU operators and MI5 officers. Seamus did valuable work, placing and operating listening devices in various locations, mostly on the border areas inside the Republic. Despite any claims to the contrary, either from the UK or Irish authorities, the FRU operated without reference to any border as such. What we were doing was clearly a breach of international law, but as far as the FRU was concerned, our need for information was more important than observing the law.

The problem with Seamus was his continuous lies and deceit. One of his most obvious 'porky pies' involved an Irish Army artillery shell that he had recovered from one of their ranges. Initially he claimed that the IRA had an artillery piece capable of firing such a shell. When the handlers had picked themselves up off the floor from laughter, and after a little persuasion, Seamus confessed that he had ventured onto the Irish Army range and 'appropriated' the abandoned shell. Seamus was an experienced smuggler and believed he knew all the safe routes for crossing the border, but had he been stopped by an RUC or UDR patrol in possession of this shell, a lot of fast talking would have been required to save his skin.

✳ ✳ ✳

Agent 3007

Another valuable agent was '3007'. Each agent inside para-military groups was given a number. The first two digits gave the location of the agent in Northern Ireland; the second two were the agent's unique identifying number. A '30' prefix signified the area controlled by the FRU's western detachment (West Det.). The infamous agent, Brian Nelson, whom you will read about later in the book, was '6137', the '61' signifying East Det. FRU.

3007 lived in Derry. He was a married man with three children, one of whom had learning difficulties. This agent was motivated almost exclusively by finance. His wife became aware that her husband was working for the FRU, and although she was 100 percent against what he was doing, she remained silent through loyalty to her husband. This lady was fearless. Once, or maybe twice a year, she would accompany her husband to his meeting with us, and in her hand there was always a cluster of unpaid bills – everything from electricity and telephone bills to the bill from Radio Rentals for the family television and video. No wonder she spent countless hours on the telephone; she knew that we would look after her talk-time later. I can remember my heart missing a beat as I spotted her walking towards the pick-up vehicle. The prospect of receiving a verbal battering from this lady was not what most handlers would consider a good afternoon's sport.

Agent 3007 was important to the FRU because he could give a political insight deep inside the republican movement at a crucial point in the embryonic stage of the political party we know today as Sinn Féin. At one point he was the treasurer for Sinn Féin in Derry. The FRU encouraged him to become involved in as many community organisations as possible. Then it set about providing him with information that could raise his profile in these organisations, for example on what grants such groups could get from the British government. In time, 3007 became an expert in getting government funding for all types of schemes, such as the Action for Community Employment (ACE) schemes, which provided jobs for the long-term unemployed. Ridiculously high unemployment levels in republican areas, mainly due to a long history of discrimination, meant that such schemes were common. Our man became recognised as someone who could get things done; soon other groups infiltrated and run by republicans came to rely upon his information. His status was helped when grant applications that should have gone into the bin didn't and were paid out in full.

3007's cover was blown when MI5 agent Michael Bethany, who was a Soviet spy, revealed his name to republicans who were fellow inmates of his in Wormwood Scrubs prison. However, FRU got the information before it reached the IRA and 3007 was relocated to Britain, with a new house and a new identity. His marriage subsequently collapsed and he is now penniless.

✳ ✳ ✳

Declan

While some top IRA members did work for the FRU, often our operators were simply 'eyes and ears' agents, people with some access and a willingness to spy on the work of known members. One such agent we will call 'Declan', a mature family man from the Cavan/Monaghan border area. Declan was a lovely, honest man, but as bright as a broken light bulb.

Declan provided good access to prominent personalities who worked and operated in the border region. He was not a 'green-booked' IRA man, ie, sworn in to the organisation on the Green Book, the training manual of the IRA. However, he was trusted by paramilitaries to the extent that vehicles he owned were often used for the movement of very interesting people around the country on 'business'. Needless to say, these vehicles were completely wired for sound. Even discreet conversations in the rear seats were recorded, and as a result a number of arms caches were located and operations were successfully attacked or frustrated, without Declan necessarily being aware of his role in the affair.

On one memorable occasion, Declan decided, for one reason or another, that he needed to initiate a meeting with his handler. He went to a public phone and dialled the number, but on hearing the bleeps which signify that money must be deposited prior to a connection being made, he was completely mystified. He hung up and tried again, with the same result. He made twenty attempts to call and the office was in uproar waiting for him to deposit a coin in the slot. But he never worked it out.

Defeated, he returned home and successfully made the call from there, and a meeting was arranged. His handler had recently explained a new pick-up procedure to Declan. This involved a 'rolling pick-up'; upon sighting the FRU van, Declan was to follow until the van pulled over. On this occasion, Declan's instructions were to meet on the Bal-lygawley roundabout at three o'clock. Declan took the directive literally and, on approaching the Ballygawley roundabout, the cover van spotted a vehicle parked on the grassy area in the middle of the roundabout, with Declan sitting patiently and nonchalantly at the wheel!

The handlers had no choice but to abort the meeting, not wishing to enter one of the busiest road junctions in Northern Ireland with every single gaping-eyed motorist staring at their agent, sitting plumb bang in the middle of the roundabout.

Despite incidents like this, Declan was a useful agent who gave us access to some high-ranking paramilitaries. Information gathered with his help was crucial in stopping a number of operations that the Provisionals had planned along the border. Frustrating operations without compromising such an agent was difficult, but a police or Army patrol just 'happening' to be in the right place at the right time could often be enough to thwart an attack. It was valuable work.

An advantage to running an agent such as Declan was that he was not viewed by the republican movement as being 'involved'. Consequently, whenever the IRA's security department convened an inquiry into a failed or compromised operation, the chances were that little attention would be paid to him, as he should have had no knowledge of the operation in the first place.

In comparison, an agent who had direct access and a 'hands--on' involvement could be difficult to control, for a number of reasons. The direct involvement of an agent in bombings and murders was a recipe for disaster. If a handler recorded the agent's activities accurately in official paperwork, he or she was storing up trouble. The ideal agent was one who had access or a role in the administration, yet did not become involved in the 'hands-on' part of the operations.

✳ ✳ ✳

It is a fact of life that no informant inside any paramilitary organisation could possibly get to the heart of that organisation without committing criminal offences, and this is where the agencies who employ such informants walk a fine line. They have to ask themselves how far they can allow such agents to go, and when does the cost become too much. Handlers in all services have recruited killers and would-be killers throughout the Troubles. This practice is unacceptable when innocent people die as a result, but it is truly appalling when members of the security forces know their agents are killing innocent people and they do nothing about it. Under Northern Ireland law, RUC informants can be given 'participation status', whereby they are allowed to commit a crime in order to prevent a greater crime taking place, but, in my book, there is no greater crime than murder.

Unfortunately, during the last thirty years a number of agents have been run and handled right up to and over the line of both the law and common humanity. Stakeknife was not alone in being encouraged to occupy a role within a paramilitary organisation that is difficult to reconcile with good practice or morality. I freely admit that in my early years in the FRU I would not have had much difficulty with some of the 'seedier' sides of certain operations, and I still believe that the FRU was working towards a better situation in Northern Ireland. However, sometime in the mid to late 1980s the 'acceptable line' of operational ethics was crossed and I began to seriously question its methodology and practices.

Chapter 4

The Agent Stakeknife

Ingram

Frederick Scappaticci grew up in the Markets area of south Belfast, the son of Daniel Scappaticci, an Italian immigrant who arrived in Belfast in the 1920s. Belfast, like Glasgow, Manchester, Dublin and other cities at the time saw a large influx of Italian families seeking a better life. There were so many Italian immigrants in the old docks area, around the Markets area of Belfast, that it was known as 'Little Italy'. The Scappaticcis ran a number of ice-cream businesses. Scappaticci was reputed to be an unruly and bad-tempered teenager, once breaking the leg of a fourteen-year-old in a row over football. Football was his passion – in 1962 he travelled to Nottingham Forest for a three-week trial but was sent home. The left-sided midfielder, although barely five-and-a-half feet tall, was highly rated by scout Johnny Carey, a former Manchester United and Irish international. However, the other Manchester – Manchester City – was Scappaticci's team and after he became an agent the FRU would often arrange tickets for him for big matches at Maine Road. It also provided good cover when Scappaticci wanted to spend a weekend with his handlers.

Scappaticci, like his father, was a republican. He was caught up in the early Troubles, and was fined for riotous behaviour in 1970. A year later he was interned with, amongst others, Francisco Notorantonio, Gerry Adams, Alex Maskey and Ivor Bell. Now working as a bricklayer, Scappaticci was twenty-five years old. Veteran Derry republican Michael Donnelly, who was also interned at Long Kesh, recalled the now-notorious Scappaticci temper in a conversation with BBC Northern Ireland journalist Vincent Kearney: 'Freddie Scap was short-tempered and quick to throw a punch ... If he had been a foot taller he would have been a dangerous bully, but as it was he usually had one or two with him when he did throw his weight about, and he didn't do much damage.'

Donnelly said Scappaticci 'hung around with the Ballymurphy team, who were led by Gerry Adams'. He was particularly touchy about his name, which many of his fellow inmates mispronounced: 'He would stamp his feet and shout, "It's Scap-a-tichi, Scap-a-f******-tichi!"' said Donnelly.

Scappaticci was released in December 1974 and became a trusted member of the Provisional IRA. He volunteered his services to British Army intelligence in 1978. Meanwhile he was working his way up through the IRA ranks. By 1980 – the year the Force Research Unit was established to centralise Army intelligence under the Intelligence Corps – Freddie Scappaticci, with guidance and help from his handlers, was firmly ensconced in the IRA's internal security department, aka the Nutting Squad.

From then until early 1996 (although there was less work for his Nutting Squad after the 1994 ceasefire), Scappaticci would have a role in investigations into suspected informers, inquiries into operations suspected of being compromised, debriefings of IRA volunteers released from questioning and vetting of potential recruits. The FRU had placed its prize asset at the centre of the IRA, at the heart of Northern Command. During my time in the FRU he was referred to as Stake, Stakeknife, Steak or Steak-Knife and sometimes as Alfredo – Italian for Freddie. By the time he was outed, Stakeknife had become the norm.

I first became aware of both his activities and the role of the FRU in those activities in the early 1980s. One evening during 1982 whilst visiting the office at Headquarters Northern Ireland, a telephone call on a source telephone, a dedicated line for agents, was taken by a colleague who was the 121 Intelligence Section duty operator. This colleague, whom we shall call 'Sam', was, like myself, inexperienced as an intelligence operative. Sam took the call from an RUC officer based at Donegall Pass RUC station. The gist of the conversation was that an individual had been arrested for drink driving and had asked the RUC desk sergeant to telephone his handlers and alert them to his predicament. The 'individual' was in fact, Freddie Scappaticci, whom the police had arrested near his home, which was on the Lower Ormeau Road, about half a mile from the Donegall Pass station in south Belfast.

Whilst Sam telephoned those responsible for the running of Stakeknife, seeking instructions, I kept the desk sergeant occupied on the phone. Throughout that evening I helped out in the office, running errands for the posse of FRU officers and handlers who had returned to their offices to deal with the developing situation. The RUC desk sergeant confirmed the identity of the arrested man as Frederick or Freddie Scappaticci; he was requested to avoid doing anything which would highlight the identity of the individual he had in custody. The name Scappaticci was not known to me in the context of the Troubles at that time. In truth, both Sam and I were curious – it was in our natures. We were trained to be nosy, to find things out that we weren't supposed to, and we were both delighted that we were allowed and trusted to remain in the background whilst a crisis was managed.

Once Scappaticci had been safely released from RUC custody without charge and the handlers had left the offices, we ran his name through the intelligence computer system 3702. His name and his activities were clearly recorded. He was identified as being closely involved in the running of the IRA's feared internal security unit and being linked to the IRA's Northern Command. It was clear to Sam and me that this was a heavy-duty source at the higher echelons of the Provisional IRA. We knew even then that to have a mole inside the Provos' own security unit was a massive coup. Sam and I were summoned the following day to a meeting with the operation officer FRU and told to keep the secret of Stakeknife's identity. At the time both of us were frankly out of our depth, unaware why the operation officer was anxious over and above normal concerns for the source's welfare. This was, however, to change.

Over the next few years I became friendly with one of Stakeknife's primary handlers, a man that I will call 'Andy'. Andy and myself were keen footballers, playing for both the local unit and in the many five-a-side competitions held on Thiepval barracks. Andy was aware that I knew the identity of his agent and was open with me concerning Stakeknife and his activities, although careful to paint Stakeknife in a positive light. I believe Andy knew even as early as the mid-1980s that this case could come back to haunt not only him but the FRU as a unit. On occasions when I suggested he be careful, he intimated that the paperwork generated would not accurately reflect much of the agent's activities, certainly not the aspects which were clearly illegal.

Stakeknife produced high-grade intelligence, much of it read at the highest levels of the political and security establishments. He was, without doubt, the jewel in the crown. The problem was, Stakeknife could only shine if he immersed himself in the activities of those he was reporting upon, including murder and other illegal acts.

Stakeknife had knowledge of some high-profile kidnap cases, many of which ended well. One is the case of supermarket magnate Ben Dunne Jnr, kidnapped by an IRA gang in south Armagh in 1981. Scappaticci was influential in saving his life, according to FRU source reports. The then chief of Dunnes Stores, aged thirty-one, was on his way to Portadown to open a new branch of the company. He was pulled from his car by armed maverick IRA men when he stopped to help at a fake accident. During Dunne's six-day ordeal, Father Dermod McCarthy met with the terror gang and later appealed on television for his release. As Father McCarthy tried to mediate, a fierce gun battle broke out between the IRA members and Garda Special Branch, who had located the terrorists' secret lair in County Louth after receiving accurate intelligence. Although Gardaí and sources close to the family said no money was paid, I have read in intelligence reports that around Stg£300,000 was handed over.

Scappaticci was also a major source in the foiled kidnap attempt on Galen Weston, a Canadian-born business tycoon and friend of Britain's Prince Charles. The Westons had set up home in Toronto, but maintained their spectacular Irish estate at Roundwood Park, a seventeenth-century castle on 245 acres in the Wicklow hills, outside Dublin. On 7 August 1983, seven terrorists approached the Westons' mansion in their bid to kidnap him. However, a fortnight earlier the FRU had passed on information from Scappaticci to Gardaí via the RUC. The seven men walked into a Garda ambush, an elaborate trap set up to give the impression that the Westons were at the estate. Weston, then forty-two, and his wife Hilary, a former Irish model, were not at home. He was playing polo with Prince Charles. He dismissed claims that it was a kidnap attempt. 'Anyone could have known I was in England,' he said at the time. 'I haven't been to Roundwood for months. The estate is run as a farm but there are some nice paintings and furniture in the house – I suppose they were after that.' Gardaí eventually convinced the Westons that the gang, which had cut telephone wires to the house, had more sinister motives and as a result the couple sold up and left Ireland.

Another kidnapping, in late 1983, would result in the deaths of a garda and an Irish Army soldier. Quinnsworth boss Don Tidey was stopped at what appeared to be a Garda checkpoint near his home in Rathfarnham, Dublin. However, a gun was put to his head as he was taken prisoner by the IRA. His nineteen-year-old son was beaten during the abduction, which was also witnessed by his thirteen-year-old daughter. After being held hostage for twenty-three days, Tidey was rescued in a joint Army–Garda operation in Ballinamore, County Leitrim, on 16 December. He was found in a dugout in a secluded wooded area under the guard of four armed men, all of whom escaped. Again, Scappaticci's information had been passed on to the Gardaí by the British authorities after a tip-off to the FRU. Trainee garda Gary

Sheehan, twenty-three, of Carrickmacross, County Monaghan, and Private Patrick Kelly, thirty-five, of Moate, County
Westmeath, were killed in the shoot-out. In 1998 IRA jail-
breaker Brendan 'Bik' McFarlane was bailed on charges connected with the kidnap of the supermarket boss.

Don Tidey and Ben Dunne, among others, owe their lives
to Freddie Scappaticci. But there were those who lost their
lives to Scappaticci in his role as tout-finder general. The difficult part for his handlers involved manoeuvring him into
the prominent and influential role as second-in-command in
the internal security unit. Intelligence given to Scappaticci by
the FRU aided his credibility within the IRA. Unfortunately,
Scappaticci's very position would inevitably involve him in
regular murders. The price, in my opinion, for his excellent
intelligence was too high – although that assessment is with
the benefit of hindsight and was not my opinion fifteen years
ago. Gradually and with a large degree of patience, Scappaticci was developed into an agent who was trusted and
respected.

From the moment I became aware of Stakeknife's identity
I wondered what had prompted an individual like this to
turn traitor and inform on his friends and comrades. A few
years after I became aware of Stakeknife's identity, Andy
informed me that Scappaticci had been a 'walk-in' – that is,
he voluntarily walked into an Army base and offered to
report information on individuals who had crossed paths
with him. Andy told me that either an individual or group
associated with the IRA had given Scappaticci a beating. This
beating to a proud man had been the Rubicon that prompted
him to turn traitor. But surely, I thought, that alone could not
be the sole motivating factor that was to fuel a long and

successful career as an agent for the British State. In conversations with handlers it became clear that Stakeknife was also motivated by personal grudges. Andy once told me that Scappaticci hated Martin McGuinness vehemently and that in all his dealings as an IRA officer connected to Northern Command his reporting of the activities of McGuinness was always full and detailed.

This dislike was aired publicly in two interviews given during in the mid-1990s to ITV's 'The Cook Report'. These give a fascinating insight into the agent's mental make-up. 'The Cook Report' had broadcast a previous programme, delving into the activities of Martin McGuinness and his involvement with the IRA. The programme examined McGuinness's dual role – his political career in Sinn Féin, and his position as an IRA commander. However, Scappaticci did not believe the programme had uncovered enough of McGuinness's activities and he sensationally decided to offer his services, under an assumed name, to journalists in the hope of really digging the dirt on McGuinness. It is unclear whether he volunteered this information with the blessing of his handlers or if he was flying solo.

Scappaticci met the journalists in the Culloden Hotel, outside Belfast. He drove there in his own car, registered in his own name. This seems frankly suicidal, although it is true that by now he was not anywhere near as active in the IRA as he had been. Journalists are generally smart creatures, skilled at identifying sources and blessed with willing sources of their own. Stakeknife was easily identified by a quick check on the registration number of his car, casually parked within the grounds of the hotel. A registration number can be checked with police sources.

The journalists were surprised that a senior republican would willingly come out into the open, even under an assumed name. This casual approach seems to imply that Scappaticci was acting with his handlers' knowledge. He would also not have wanted to upset his employers with this type of activity if it was not authorised. This man had made a career from not making mistakes – you do not survive over two decades as an agent in the IRA by being casual and reckless. This action seems reckless at best, although it was highly unlikely any republicans would have been in the hotel, or would have had access to the journalists he was meeting. It is impossible to be sure what Scappaticci's motivations were.

Below is a transcript of parts of Scappaticci's conversations with the 'Cook Report' team. He is remarkably outspoken in his allegations, which are denied by McGuinness and others. He makes a number of statements which are inconsistent with facts, for example his claim that he was no longer in the IRA. He also makes several errors or slips of the mind regarding details, mentioning the 'five-man' Army council rather than seven, forgetting that Northern Command covered eleven counties rather than nine, ie, the 'war zone' – the six counties of Northern Ireland and the five bordering counties in the Republic of Ireland. These slips, of course, undermine his validity as a credible witness on any issue, but despite this, the interview does give us Scappaticci's own voice and attitudes, his vindictiveness, and his hatred of McGuinness. Of course, Scappaticci was covering his own back, presenting his own case to his interviewers, but I include it here to give the flavour of his thinking at this time. I would caution readers to be circumspect regarding the allegations made by Scappaticci below. Because of his unreliability we have removed names.

The first interview took place on 26 August 1993 at the Culloden Hotel in Cultra, County Down, about six miles from Belfast. TV director and producer Clive Entwistle and award-winning ex-*Daily Mirror* reporter Frank Thorne were with former *Daily Mirror* crime correspondent Sylvia Jones. 'The Cook Report' had earlier broadcast allegations that Martin McGuinness was involved in the murder of FRU agent Frank Hegarty in Donegal, an agent handled by me whose case is dealt with in more detail in Chapter 6.

'Cook Report' team: *You've known our friend a long …*

Scappaticci: McGuinness? Oh, I know him very well. I know him about twenty years, you know. Basically, see the thing you were putting across on the programme the other night, that he's in charge of the IRA. He's not as such. It's a technical thing, right. The IRA's split in two. There's another command, a Southern Command. He's in charge of Northern Command. He's the Northern Command OC. There's a Southern Command, it has nothing to do with the Northern Command. The Northern Command basically takes in the nine counties of Ulster, right. He controls all of that. He's also on the IRA Army Council. There's a five-man Army Council. He's one of them. Nothing happens in Northern Command that he doesn't okay, and I mean nothing. Now, he's nothing to do with England. See what happens in England, he's nothing to do with that. The person who controls England is a south Armagh fella, right?

'Cook Report' team: *So who would be responsible for [the bombing of] Warrington?*

Scappaticci: A fella called [A] in south Armagh. He actually controls all aspects of what happens in England and on the Continent. Him and another guy called [B]. [B] is an ex-Belfast fella now living in Carlingford, right. They are the people who control what goes on in England.

'Cook Report' team: *Does McGuinness have anything to do with that though?*

Scappaticci: Well, he would have an input obviously.

'Cook Report' team: *He's involved?*

Scappaticci: Well, I mean, yes. He's involved as such that he's an IRA man.

'Cook Report' team: *And he's on the [Army] Council?*

Scappaticci: Oh, yes, he's on the IRA Army Council. They have to give the go-ahead for what happens in England, right. Basically, I felt see, the programme itself, it didn't go deeply enough. If you want to take in Martin McGuinness, you have to take in a couple of other people.

'Cook Report' team: *That was one of the problems we had. We have a lot of evidence on people like [C] and so on.*

Scappaticci: No, no, no, not [C]. [C] is nothing. I'm talking about the likes of a guy called [D] … I was explaining to Frank, McGuinness is on the IRA Army Council. He also controls the Northern Command which takes in the nine counties of Ulster. That was formed in 1977 by Ivor Bell, split Northern/Southern Command. There's a five-man Army Council which McGuinness is part of. Nothing happens in Northern Command that McGuinness doesn't okay, but there's another person there too, who's, I would say, more militarily involved in Northern Command. He's his [McGuinness's] adjutant, a fella called [D] from Beechmount. Do you know of him?

'Cook Report' team: *We know of him.*

Scappaticci: Anything that would happen, [D] would have the say-so. Right? Would okay it with McGuinness. He meets McGuinness once or twice a week in Belfast. This is a regular arrangement, right? McGuinness would come to Belfast. Used to be McGuinness would come to Belfast on a Tuesday. Every week. He stayed for two days. Him and [D] would do what they have to do. But what they've basically done is, they've cut up the Northern Command area, right? [D]'s basically looking after Belfast. [D], since he come out of jail – he's out of jail almost seven years – he's Adjutant of Northern Command, operates under McGuinness. He [D] more or less controls Down, Armagh, Tyrone. They sort of broke it up into two halves. McGuinness would look after the top half, Derry …

'Cook Report' team: *Do you mind if I make some notes?*

Scappaticci: No, that's okay. Derry, Donegal. They more or less split up the Northern Command into two. It's to facilitate both of the … because McGuinness, obviously from Derry, looks after Derry, Donegal.

'Cook Report' team: *But is McGuinness in overall control of Northern Command?*

Scappaticci: He is the Northern Command OC. There's a five-man Army Council, he's one of them. Adams is another.

'Cook Report' team: *He wouldn't be responsible for English operations, but he would be part of the team that sanctioned them?*

Scappaticci: What happens is, I'll explain the situation to you, right? The IRA Army Council says: This is what our strategy should be for the next year. We'll have to do this, blah, blah. We think the operations should be in England or the Continent or whatever. That then filters down to the people who control it, who I told you is [A] and a guy called [B], right, who's living in Carlingford at the minute. He moved out of Belfast.

Scappaticci: ... Now you see that guy Rob Friars that was caught in England with a bomb about six or seven weeks ago? Remember he was caught at the bus stop in London? Cannon fodder, know what I mean? But a big mate of this guy [D]. And it was actually [D] who recommended him for the England thing to [A], as [D] moves in and out of the south Armagh area a lot. See, if they are carrying out any interrogations of so-called informers, that's where they do it, in that area, mostly. The likes of Derry people would be done in Donegal, but it would be the same team that would do the whole lot, right, and it's under the control of [D] and they're the ones that do that type of thing. So as I was trying to explain, by just saying McGuinness, I don't think you went deeply enough into it, you know what I mean? It done no harm and exposed him [McGuinness] for what he is. And, see that woman that came on [Rose Hegarty], she was right in what she was saying, like, he is an evil person.

'Cook Report' team: *Mrs Hegarty?*

Scappaticci: Yes, because he gave the go-ahead for Frank Hegarty, right? Well, I'll tell you what I know about it, right ... There was weapons caught in Donegal. It was 150 rifles caught. Hegarty was the one that gave the information on that. He was then taken out, brought to England and missed his common-law wife. So he kept phoning back. So McGuinness got on the phone and says, "Come back, you'll be okay, blah, blah." Convinced him he'd be okay, convinced the mother. He [Hegarty] then came home and McGuinness was the instrument of him being taken away and shot.

'Cook Report' team: *How do you know this?*

Scappaticci: I know it because for a long time I was at the heart of things. I'm no longer at the heart of things, right. Haven't been for two or three years, right. But I know what I'm talking about, right.

'Cook Report' team: *When you say you were at the heart of things, how close were you to McGuinness?*

Scappaticci: Well, let's say I served on the same thing he's on.

'Cook Report' team: *The Army Council?*

Scappaticci: No. The Northern Command.

'Cook Report' team: *So you were part of the decision team to get Hegarty then?*

Scappaticci: No, no, no. You see, that's a totally different thing. You have to know the workings of the IRA to know what happens.

'Cook Report' team: *What is McGuinness up to at the moment?*

Scappaticci: Well, he's still Northern Command OC, but there was a decision taken four year ago that McGuinness was going to step back from things on the military side and take a political role.

'Cook Report' team: *Why was that?*

Scappaticci: Sinn Féin, the popularity they had in the early eighties started to wane and they were realising this. McGuinness is fairly popular in Derry because he won the election up there and all that, so what was decided was that he should have a bigger role alongside Adams, to try to get Sinn Féin going and put gee-up into it, right? So they were grooming yer man [D] to take over as OC of Northern Command and what you see now is that [D] has basically taken the reins of Northern Command and McGuinness has more or less stepped out. McGuinness still has to okay everything but he's more or less stepped back and is more in a political role. But he's still in the IRA. Deep there, like, you know. Very deep.

'Cook Report' team: *Were you side-by-side with McGuinness?*

Scappaticci: No, no, no. He's the type of person you don't get side-by-side with. He's a very cold person. He doesn't have friends within the IRA. He has what he calls comrades. He doesn't have friends as such. He frowns on womanising, he frowns on drinking – a very moralistic person.

Scappaticci is asked about getting his story on screen.

Scappaticci: Well, you see, things that I would be giving you would be people's lives being taken, you see, that he [McGuinness] gave the go-ahead for doing it, you know. Bombing city centres, he gave the go-ahead for doing it. Decisions are taken, Army Council makes a decision, then there's a Northern Command meeting called and the Northern Command meeting is told, "This is the *craic*, we're gonna concentrate on city-centre bombs. This is what we have to do." And there would be a one-day coordinated strike – that's what they call it – in the Six Counties of bombs being put out in different towns, different cities for mass devastation. The reason they come back on this seventies thing of bombs in the city centres is because they see how hard it is hitting the British government moneywise, plus the effect it has. Now, you notice there's not many British soldiers being killed now, because they haven't got the expertise in Belfast to do it, the likes of that. Okay, they have in south Armagh and places like that, but they change their tactics every now and again.

At this point, the transcript notes that Scappaticci says that people thought the first post-election bomb in the city of London was a reaction to Peter Brooke, but that in fact it had been planned weeks earlier.

Scappaticci: The media love to have these theories, that the IRA are masterminds. They're not. Okay, sometimes things fall into place and they can claim afterwards, "we did it for that reason," but they didn't do it for that reason.

Here the tape runs out on the first meeting. Clive Entwistle takes a shorthand note of what is said next: Scappaticci claimed that Martin McGuinness would be paid £20 a week, plus expenses, have a car and driver provided, expenses for petrol, etc. If he went into a bar or local butcher's he would get given drinks or meat free. So he lives for free.

Scappaticci: He is ruthless. I can say this unequivocally. He has the final say on an informer, whether that person lives or dies. If it is an IRA volunteer who admits it [informing] he is court-martialled. Only two key people on the Army Council – that is, Martin McGuinness and Gerry Kelly, who acts as Adjutant General – make the decision. If he is not an IRA volunteer, it is Martin McGuinness who gives the say-so. It just needs McGuinness, he has the final say. That is 100 percent. If McGuinness is not about, [E] gives the order.

Hegarty was an affront. He [McGuinness] took it very personally. There is something quite wrong with his head. He talks to you very quietly, very softly, but he would think nothing about putting us [the three in the car] down. He would be praying in chapel one minute, go outside and think nothing about ordering a shooting. Before Hegarty was shot I knew about it. A friend of mine was to interrogate Hegarty, but McGuinness, [A] and [F] interrogated him. McGuinness ordered his shooting.

The reason they gave was because of the arms shipment found in Sligo. He had to be made an example. McGuinness was instrumental in getting him back. He engineered getting him back and talking to him on the phone. He [Hegarty] was knocking around [in the early 1970s]. Ivor Bell, ex-chief of staff, blocked Hegarty coming in. Bell didn't like his [Official IRA] background. He just didn't fancy him. When Bell went Hegarty started working for a fella from Derry. He's now in Strabane … Hegarty started helping on the QM [quartermaster] side and got more deeply involved.

'Cook Report' team: *Clive asks how big a blow the arms find was.*

Scappaticci: Jesus, it was a major blow, that arms find, because at that time we didn't have many. Before that there was only a small amount of arms. It only came out then that there was all this stuff from Libya. It wasn't McGuinness who felt responsible, it was just that Hegarty had been responsible [for Gardaí finding more than 100 weapons in Roscommon and Sligo] and something had to be done.

'Cook Report' team: *Clive asks about current strategy.*

Scappaticci: All plans have to be sanctioned by McGuinness. Any change in strategy would have to be made by McGuinness. They are very sensitive about publicity. There was a groundswell recently to shoot unionist politicians like Sammy Wilson and SDLP. But Army Council will not let them do it.

'Cook Report' team: *Scappaticci is asked why he had left the organisation after 22 years.*

Scappaticci: There are more things in life than killing.

'Cook Report' team: *Had he killed?*

Scappaticci: No answer.

'Cook Report' team: *Clive asks more questions.*

Scappaticci: A culture has built up. McGuinness is now famous. He gets a kick out of it, out of killing. Where would he be today? Still a butcher's boy. Where would Gerry Adams be? Working behind a bar. He was a barman. I would say if there was a free vote tomorrow it would be a massive yes to stop the violence. Adams would stop it but McGuinness would not. I have been at meetings with him, Adams and Sean Maguire, and the whole atmosphere of the armed struggle and how it was going to be developed was discussed. I was at two meetings. He [McGuinness] is a cold person. One minute he would be in church and next he would say 'stiff him'.

We tried to get conversation going again, but he just wasn't interested. All he wanted to do was get away – so did we.

'Cook Report' team: *Clive is told that Scappaticci attended meetings to discuss targeting Wimbledon, Buckingham Palace and the attack on Downing Street. Killing Thatcher was also discussed.*

Scappaticci: But she was too well guarded. You might get a meeting where everything is in the melting pot.

'Cook Report' team: *Was McGuinness involved in the mortar bomb attack on Downing Street?*

Scappaticci: [A] and [B] worked out the strategy. Rob Friars welded up the mortar. They use people not known in England who can come and go unnoticed, who are not going to break. Bombings ... would come personally from Northern Command, so McGuinness would automatically know about them. If [A] or [B] wanted, say, six men who were unknown, they would go to McGuinness who would go around the local OCs in Northern Command and ask them to find six suitable men. They would be told to say they had got disillusioned with the organisation and dropped out, or say they had got a job in Germany or Dublin or wherever. We used to take people across [to Britain] in fishing boats but I don't know how they travel there now.

Scappaticci says the meeting has gone on too long and ends that meeting.

Next meeting: 28 August 1993, east Belfast.

Present: Clive Entwistle, Sylvia Jones, Frank Thorne and 'Jack', aka Freddie Scappaticci.

Scappaticci: Hegarty came back because he was given assurances that he would be safe. You think life is sweet when those assurances come from the top man – Martin McGuinness. He gave his word of honour. McGuinness told Frank and his family he would be taken over the border to meet three prominent people in the IRA Army Council. McGuinness was part of the Army Council who first interrogated Hegarty, court-martialled him and then ordered him to be shot. Inside the IRA it was known from the moment those guns were found that Frankie was 'going for his tea'. That was it. He was a dead man. It's not important who pulled the trigger. McGuinness wouldn't dirty his hands with that. Hegarty was court-martialled because he was an IRA volunteer. He threw himself on the mercy of the Army Council. They went into another room, said, 'No – take him out and give him it.' A real kangaroo court. They would have blindfolded him and assured him they were taking him home, then would have taken him from the car and told him to keep walking … a bullet in the back of the head. Four bullets is normal, usually by two people so that they are both implicated in the murder.

On McGuinness giving Hegarty and his family the word that Frank would be safe, Scappaticci scoffed:

Scappaticci: See if someone in the IRA says, 'I swear to God,' or, 'I swear on my mother's life,' then you know you are getting double-crossed. That's the code word. You say, right – bolt. Bolt.

He said McGuinness would not normally be personally involved in interrogations.

Scappaticci: In the final analysis in the Northern Command, he [McGuinness] would have to give the go-ahead for them to be shot.

Entwistle: *How many executions would you say McGuinness has authorised over the years?*

Scappaticci: How many executions have there been, you tell me? I can't keep a score of them. Forty? Fifty? Sixty? A hundred? You look at every British soldier shot, every policeman shot, every booby trap or whatever. McGuinness is ultimately responsible for all of it. It's all under his control.

Entwistle: *So the thousands of people who have died, McGuinness is responsible for their deaths?*

Scappaticci: He's responsible for the majority. If you met him in his role in Sinn Féin, he is a nice plausible person. But in his role in the IRA, he is a cold, ruthless person. He sends a shiver down your back. At IRA meetings, he is businesslike. You don't get much chit-chat out of him.

Entwistle: *How damaging was the arms find? How damaging was that information which Frank [Hegarty] had given at that time?*

Scappaticci: The decision was taken for McGuinness to be more political. Sinn Féin had started to decline. They thought that Adams had too much of a workload and needed more help. And there was also schemes brought forward for the

IRA to contribute to help pull them back together again. The IRA appointed a person in Belfast and his sole job was to look after Sinn Féin/IRA-type things – coordinate publicity campaigns, etc. If Sinn Féin wasn't doing too well in an area, the IRA could be deployed in that area to do various things, to work alongside Sinn Féin.

Entwistle: *To whip up support?*

Scappaticci: Oh, aye.

Entwistle: *Was it done as threats?*

Scappaticci: Part of this coordination would have been 'civil administration' – that is, the people who knee-cap people, baseball-bat people who break legs, arms, is what their 'civil administration' is. There you are. The IRA made a conscious decision along with Sinn Féin to clean up the Divis Flats because of the crime and drug dealing. An IRA man was put in to call on people to band together and make the Divis Flats a hoods-free area. The hoods showed out and the IRA moved in and knee-capped four or five people. Then they gave a particular drug-dealing family forty-eight hours to get out of Belfast or be 'stiffed'. They left. The Lower Falls became quiet. Sinn Féin got their act together and got two seats in the Lower Falls.

Entwistle: *People have told us the link between Sinn Féin and the IRA is inseparable.*

Scappaticci: It's inseparable. Many Sinn Féin councillors are in the IRA. Martin McGuinness is on the IRA Army Council. [He names others but adds that some councillors are not IRA.] If you look at the IRA – you look at the 1970s – it's still the same people who are coordinating and controlling things who were operating in the seventies and they are set in their ways.

Scappaticci was more nervous this time. He cut the meeting short. His claims were clearly designed to damage the republican movement, and in particular Martin McGuinness, at a time when republicans were moving towards calling a cease-fire and kick-starting the peace process. His animosity towards McGuinness is clear and not in any way guarded, and his intent is evidently to place pressure upon McGuinness at what was a very delicate time, with the fledgling peace process still finding its feet. If this meeting with the journalist was authorised by FRU operations, it would seem to be an attempt to destabilise the buds of peace from flourishing by the very people who are invested with the responsibility to establish peace. If it was not authorised, it is transparent evidence of one element of the agent's motivation.

What makes Scappaticci's conversations with these journalists truly remarkable was that Scappaticci had told his handler in the FRU that the man who actually pulled the trigger on the gun that killed Frank Hegarty was none other than Scappaticci himself. The FRU were well aware that he would be involved in the interrogation of Hegarty. One FRU agent had killed another. Hegarty could have been saved, but somewhere a decision had been taken that it was better for him to die to help maintain Scappaticci's position. The Gardaí could have rescued Hegarty if they had been given details from the northern side of the border, but that information was never passed on. Coincidentally, his demise saved the State quite a lot of money in pension and resettlement payments.

After the 'Cook Report' programme was broadcast, Martin McGuinness hit back at his accusers. In an interview with the *Belfast Telegraph* on 25 August 1993 the Sinn Féin man, clearly angry, rejected all the allegations levelled against him. He said the programme was 'tabloid journalism of the worst kind – sleaze, based on perjurers, people prepared to be used as stooges of the British.' The allegations in the report were 'inconsistent and could not be true,' he insisted. Referring to one claim that he (McGuinness) had been present when people were held against their will, he said the claim was 'absolute lies'. He went on: 'There is no way I would have taken part in anything of that nature. They are total and absolute lies. I knew nothing about it.' The reporters asked him about allegations from Frank Hegarty's mother, Rose, and McGuinness responded: 'Of all the people [interviewed] she was the one that came across as the most plausible but I am afraid she is somewhat confused about what happened at the time.' Mr McGuinness said that her allegation that he had guaranteed her son's safety if he returned to Northern Ireland were wrong and he claimed that he had in fact warned Hegarty that he was 'very fearful of his life if he returned to Ireland'. Referring to the programme he said it was 'British black propaganda' and added: 'It is part of a dirty tricks campaign which I believe will fail.' He was immediately backed up by the party president Gerry Adams who told the *Belfast Telegraph*: 'It was a programme full of lies and innuendo with Roger Cook manipulating political opponents, self-confessed liars and grieving relatives.'

✳ ✳ ✳

There were other victims of Scappaticci, John Joe Magee and the Nutting Squad. Some of those victims were informers. Some were not. But the following people also died while

Army intelligence ran the man behind the interrogations, the beatings, the torture and the shootings. My experience of handling agents in Northern Ireland suggests that Freddie Scappaticci would have been involved in the majority of the murders listed. But it would also suggest that he would have had knowledge of most of these deaths, when and where they were to take place. The British State therefore could also have been aware of many of these killings.

The killing of a relative as an informer was always a massive stigma for a republican family, a black mark that would continue for generations. The IRA has recently been conducting investigations into a number of executions by the Nutting Squad, at the behest of relatives who have always insisted that their loved ones were unjustly murdered. They have evidently known for some time that the wrong people were killed on some occasions.

The discovery of informers in their ranks was also very dispiriting and demoralising for IRA members. It was very much in the interests of British intelligence agencies to sow alarm, despondency and paranoia in IRA ranks by having a regular supply of informers allegedly 'unmasked'.

Considering what is now known about Scappaticci, it is likely that some of these people were killed to protect him, to throw the IRA off his scent, as his information would have compromised many IRA operations. There were thirty-five victims while Scappaticci worked in the Nutting Squad:

Paul Valente, a thirty-three-year-old married father of four, was from Stanhope Drive in Unity Flats, Belfast. He was shot dead on 14 November 1980 by the Nutting Squad. His body was dumped in the loyalist Highfield estate, and republicans claimed he was killed by loyalists, but it later emerged that he was killed by the IRA. It was also claimed that he had told RUC Special Branch about an IRA mole inside the police. I believe Scappaticci would have been involved in this inquiry, giving the security forces vital information.

Maurice Gilvarry, twenty-four years old, was abducted, tortured and shot dead by the IRA. His body was dumped on a road in south Armagh. Gilvarry, from Butler Street in north Belfast, was found on 20 January 1981. He had been providing information to the security forces for a number of years. His information had led to the deaths of three IRA members and a Protestant civilian in an SAS ambush at a post office in north Belfast in June 1978.

Patrick Gerard Trainor, a twenty-eight-year-old father of three from Farset Walk in Divis, Lower Falls, west Belfast. His body was found dumped on waste ground off the Glen Road in the city on 22 February 1981. His family denied claims that he had been an informer.

Vincent Robinson, twenty-nine, a father of two from Suffolk in west Belfast, was found dead in a rubbish chute in Divis Flats on 26 June 1981. He had been shot once in the head. His family and the priest Father Denis Faul denied he was an informer. Father Faul said, 'Vincent Robinson was not murdered because he was an informer, for he was not. The accusation … is patently false.'

Anthony Braniff, twenty-seven, from Ardoyne in north Belfast, was a senior member of the Provisional IRA. His body was found dumped at Odessa Street in the Falls Road area on 27 September 1981. His relatives vehemently denied that he had worked for the security forces, a denial they maintain to this day. It was not unusual for the FRU to target senior republicans in this way – to get their agents to target such people as informers. Based on information from Scappaticci, the IRA later issued a statement claiming that Braniff was an informer. Braniff's father, David, was murdered by the UVF eight years later. The IRA have recently issued an apology and stated that Anthony Braniff was not an informer.

John Torbett, twenty-nine, was shot at his home in Horn Drive in Lenadoon on 2 January 1982, after defying an IRA exclusion order, an order to go into exile indefinitely. He died in hospital from his injuries on 19 January. His family denied that the father of four young children had worked for the security forces, and the RUC stated that the accusation was 'totally without foundation'.

Seamus Morgan, a twenty-four-year-old father of four, was from Dungannon, County Tyrone. In February 1982 Morgan, an IRA member, who had been an election worker for the hunger striker Bobby Sands, had moved to County Monaghan, claiming his life had been threatened by the security forces. He was abducted by members of the IRA's internal security unit, questioned and shot dead. His body was found dumped near Forkhill, south Armagh, on 6 March 1982. His family and close friends denied he had worked for the security forces.

Patrick Scott, twenty-seven, was from Ramoan Drive in Andersonstown. His body was found near Dunville Street in the Lower Falls area of west Belfast on 3 April 1982. His legs and hands were tied, his eyes were taped shut and he had been shot a number of times in the head. Scott, a former member of the IRA, had told family members that he had been accused of being an informer and had gone to the IRA leadership to protest his innocence. His family still deny he was an informer.

James Young, forty-one, was an IRA member from Portaferry, County Down. His body was found dumped near Crossmaglen, south Armagh, on 13 February 1984. Young had worked for the RUC for a number of years and had successfully 'jarked' (made inoperable or fitted with tracking devices) a number of weapons used by the IRA in Belfast. He had been shot several times in the head.

Brian McNally, twenty-five, was an IRA member from Beech Lodge Road in Warrenpoint, south Down. His body was found dumped on the side of a road near Meigh in south Armagh on 26 July 1984. He had been tortured for a number of days by the internal security unit, who had broken both his arms and crushed his fingers. McNally, who had claimed in a *Republican News* article several weeks earlier that he had been beaten up by police, had vehemently denied being an informer. He was shot several times. His family insist he was not an informer.

John Corcoran, a forty-five-year-old father of eight from Ballyvolac, County Cork, was a senior member of the IRA in

Munster. His body was dumped in a field near Ballincolig on 23 March 1985. He had worked as an informer for the Gardaí for up to ten years. It has been suggested that Corcoran was sacrificed to save another garda informer, Seán O'Callaghan. O'Callaghan told gardaí that Corcoran was being interrogated in County Kerry. Corcoran's garda handler has strenuously denied that Corcoran was sacrificed.

Kevin Coyle, a twenty-four-year-old father of three, confessed to being an informer for the security forces in one of the Nutting Squad's notorious taped confessions, which was later given to his family. He was taken from his home in Deanery Street in Derry city on 21 February 1985. His body was found in the city's Bogside area two days later. Coyle had told a Sinn Féin press conference earlier in February that he had refused to work for the security forces.

Catherine and Gerard Mahon were murdered on 8 September 1985. Their deaths are examined elsewhere in this book.

Damien McCrory, a twenty-year-old from Strabane in County Tyrone, was found with two bullet wounds to his head on 7 October 1985. Damien, one of eleven children whose parents were both dead, was of low intelligence. His family denied claims by the IRA that he had worked for the security forces. The IRA however, who had questioned him for almost two days before his death, said he had confessed to working for the RUC. Family members pointed out that Damien was educationally subnormal and easily misled. His death angered many republicans in Strabane at the time.

Frank Hegarty was murdered on 25 May 1986. His murder is dealt with in detail elsewhere in this book.

Patrick Murray was a thirty-year-old IRA member from the Short Strand area of east Belfast. His body was found in an entry in the Clonard area of west Belfast in the early hours of 15 August 1986. His legs and hands were tied and his eyes taped shut, and he had been shot three times in the head. His family vehemently denied that he was an informer. The IRA said he had confessed during a 'trial' to working for the security forces for eight years.

David McVeigh, forty-one, was a married father of three from Lurgan in County Armagh, and a member of the IRA. He was abducted by the IRA on 5 September 1986, questioned and tortured for five days and shot on 10 September. His body was found near Carlingford, just inside Northern Ireland. His head was covered with black polythene and his hands were tied with bandages. His family denied he was an informer.

Charles McIlmurray was a thirty-two-year-old father of two from Slemish Way in Andersonstown, west Belfast. His body was found in the back of a van near the checkpoint at Killeen, south Armagh, on 12 April 1987. He had been shot twice in the back of the head. His face was covered with a black plastic bag and his hands were tied behind his back. An IRA member, McIlmurray had worked for the RUC and had admitted this to Dungannon priest Father Denis Faul. He believed he was covered by an IRA amnesty and agreed to confess. His wife was pregnant at the time. Asked by the *Irish News* about the murder, Sinn Féin president Gerry Adams said: 'I think that Mr McIlmurray, like anyone else living in west Belfast, knows that the consequences for informing is death.'

Thomas Wilson, thirty-five, was a member of the Official IRA who the Provisionals alleged had been passing information to the security forces. His body was found near Rodney Parade, west Belfast, on 24 June 1987. His family denied he was a police informer.

Eamonn Maguire, thirty-three, from Finglas in Dublin, was alleged by the IRA to have worked for the Gardaí. He was questioned for six days by the IRA's internal security unit. His body was found in south Armagh on 1 September 1987. His family denied he was an informer and said the father of two hadn't been involved with the IRA for a number of years. The IRA however claimed he had compromised a number of their operations in the Republic.

Anthony McKiernan, a forty-four-year-old father of four, was from Stanfield Row in the Markets area of south Belfast. His body was found dumped in Mica Street in the Beechmount area of the Falls Road, west Belfast. He had been shot in the head. In a statement, the IRA said he had been a member of the organisation between 1971 and 1987 before being dismissed for 'misconduct'. McKiernan was known to Scappaticci as they were from the same area. Scappaticci was among those who interrogated McKiernan before he was shot dead on 19 January 1988. His family has always insisted he wasn't an informer.

Joseph Fenton, thirty-five, from west Belfast, was murdered on 26 February 1989. His murder is examined in more detail elsewhere in this book.

John McAnulty, a forty-eight-year-old road haulier, was abducted from a pub near Dundalk, County Louth, on 17 July 1989. His body was found dumped near Cullaville the next day. Scappaticci tortured McAnulty by beating him with his fists and stubbing cigarette ends all over his body. McAnulty 'confessed' to working for the RUC for seventeen years. Friends denied the claims, one of which was that his information had led to the arrest of Raymond McCreesh, an IRA man who died on the 1981 hunger strike at the Maze Prison.

Paddy Flood, twenty-nine, 'confessed' to being an informer and his body was found dumped near Newtownhamilton on 26 July 1990. Paddy Flood was not an informer, for the FRU, the police or anyone else. His wife has consistently denied that Flood, probably one of the IRA's most lethal members, was an informer. She deserves to know that he wasn't. Flood, from Tyrconnell Street in Derry city, had been involved in a number of operations against the security forces in the city. It is my belief that his death was a result of work by the security forces, working in conjunction with other agents inside the Provisional IRA.

Ruari Finnis, twenty-one, also from Derry, was another IRA own goal. Finnis's body was found dumped behind shops in the Creggan estate on 6 June 1991. His hands were tied behind his back and he wore a blindfold. I do not believe

Finnis was a security force agent – any compromised operations he may have been on for the IRA were almost certainly detected via electronic surveillance rather than human intelligence sources. His family deny he was an informer. The IRA say Finnis, from Harberton Park in the Waterside, confessed to working for the security forces. But who was asking the questions?

John Dignam, **Gregory Burns** and **Aidan Starrs** were found murdered on 1 July 1992. Their deaths are dealt with elsewhere in this book.

Robin Hill was a twenty-two-year-old IRA member from Ardmore Park in Coalisland, County Tyrone. His body was found at Beechmount Gardens, west Belfast, on 12 August 1992. His hands were tied, his eyes were taped shut and his body was dressed in a white boiler suit. He had been shot twice in the back of the head. The IRA said he was an informer. His family denied the claims.

Gerard Holmes, thirty-five, was from Moore Street in Derry city. His bound body was found dumped in the Creggan estate on 22 November 1992. His family vehemently denied he had worked for the security forces as the IRA claimed, even after receiving a so-called taped 'confession'. A relative was quoted in the *Derry Journal* as saying: 'The contents of the tape are not proof of our brother's guilt. In fact the reverse is the case. The tape lasts approximately two minutes and contains nothing that suggests Gerry had been an informer at any time.'

Christopher Harte, twenty-four, was from Dermott Hill Parade in west Belfast. He was married with one child. His hooded body, with hands tied behind his back, was found dumped near Castlederg, County Tyrone, on 12 February 1993. He had been held by the IRA's security unit for six days before his death. Was Harte an informer? The security forces may have wanted it to appear that way – murder conspiracy charges against him were reduced and he was granted bail before receiving a suspended prison sentence. This tactic was often employed to cast suspicion on IRA members who were not informers, deliberately making it appear that they were. Police knew who killed Harte within hours of his body being found.

James Gerard Kelly was a senior IRA member from Maghera in County Derry. The building worker was found shot in the head and body on 25 March 1993. The IRA alleged the twenty-five-year-old had been an informer for the security forces. His family denied the claims.

John Mulhern, twenty-three, was from Nansen Street in the Falls Road area of west Belfast. His body, dressed in a blue boiler suit and with his hands tied, was found about twelve miles from Castlederg, just inside Northern Ireland, on 23 June 1993. He had been questioned by the IRA security unit for a week.

Michael Brown was a twenty-three-year-old IRA member from County Leitrim. His body was found at the rear of Pat's Parlour bar on the Omeath–Newry Road on 29 April 1994. The IRA claimed he had worked for RUC Special Branch in

Downpatrick. His body was dressed in a blue boiler suit and his hands were tied behind his back. The IRA had questioned him for a week before shooting him in the head.

Caroline Moreland, thirty-four, from Beechmount Grove, west Belfast, was the second woman to die at the hands of the Nutting Squad. Her body was found on 17 July 1994 at a secluded border road at Cloughmore, County Fermanagh. She had three children. The IRA claimed she had worked for the security forces for two years.

✳ ✳ ✳

Scappaticci has made repeated denials since his exposure as the British agent Stakeknife. These denials are to be expected, if for no other reason than to protect both his own and his family's reputation within the close republican community. Early in the evening on the Monday after Scappaticci had been named as Stakeknife in three leading newspapers, I was at Heathrow airport, having just given evidence to the Bloody Sunday inquiry in London. I received a phone call from Rosie Cowan, a journalist with the *Guardian* newspaper. Rosie wanted to know what developments could be expected over the coming days and weeks. She was astounded when I predicted that Scappaticci would return home in the next few days and attempt to 'brass-neck' his way out of his predicament. Scappaticci returned home some forty-eight hours later, professing his innocence, and that was when the charade started.

At this point I want to make it abundantly clear that Scappaticci is not entirely responsible for the misery that has been caused by the agent Stakeknife. The FRU must be held to account for its involvement in this killing machine. The fact that Scappaticci was an agent of the state is to be celebrated; the callous and immoral orders given by the FRU should not. While some of Scappaticci's crimes might be covered by the Good Friday Agreement, the same cannot be said of the FRU, which, I believe, will never be brought to task for its involvement in state-sponsored murder. Terrorism is wrong. State-sponsored terrorism is equally wrong, end of story.

Chapter 5

Fear and Hypocrisy:
The Nutting Squad

Ingram/Harkin

'I'd rather have gone down for life imprisonment for something I did not do than spend an hour alone in a room with Freddie Scappaticci. When Freddie Scappaticci was in town, you made yourself scarce, very scarce. There had always been talk that even if you had not done anything wrong, Scap could get you to confess to whatever he wanted.'

Kevin Fulton, ex-IRA volunteer and FRU agent, in conversation with Ingram and Harkin.

In common with all disciplined organisations, the Provisional Irish Republican Army required a specialist unit to investigate breaches of discipline and enforce rules and regulations. This was the internal security unit, the notorious 'Nutting Squad', aligned to General Headquarters (GHQ) staff which had responsibility for the thirty-two counties. The unit had a role in clearing new recruits for the IRA, although its primary function was to collect and collate material on failed or compromised operations and on suspect or compromised individuals. Information would be extracted from a variety of sources, such as:

- Fellow volunteers or members of the general community. This type of information could be as basic as someone being seen entering an unknown vehicle in an unfamiliar area, using a public telephone on a regular basis, or having and spending money not in keeping with the individual's apparent means.
- Identification of a pattern involving one or more volunteers who participated in failed or compromised operations. If a particular unit suffered losses of equipment or manpower due to compromises, then that unit, and anybody who would, or may, have had knowledge of its operations, was suspect until such time as the compromise could be explained or a leak identified.
- Debriefing sessions of all members who had been arrested or questioned by the security forces.
- The IRA's own network of agents and sources. These agents could be police officers, telephone workers, civil servants and so on. To give one example, an agent who worked in social security or tax matters would have access to the financial records of an individual, and these records could be used to confront someone who was spending beyond their obvious means.

The internal security unit was augmented at local-unit level by volunteers responsible for day-to-day security issues, normally working to the officer commanding the local unit. It was usually at local level that the first suspicions of an individual occurred, when the level of compromised operations was above that which could be reasonably expected.

The internal security unit was pivotal to the smooth running of the IRA, and was bound to be specifically targeted for penetration by British intelligence forces. The British State put a lot of effort into penetrating the IRA on an intelligence level. Britain has always perceived the IRA as a threat to its integrity. There are other organisations and states that also see the IRA as a threat and consequently they also target the IRA. The Irish Republic has been extremely successful in penetrating the movement.

For whatever reason, the IRA kept the nucleus of this unit – John Joe Magee, an ex-British Special Boat Squadron member, and Freddie Scappaticci – intact for well over twenty years. This was a major mistake. In the equivalent unit in the FRU, internal security staff were rotated frequently, often at a moment's notice, limiting any potential penetration to a defined period of time. With Stakeknife in place, the IRA effectively had no internal security.

Internal IRA investigation

If a unit had been penetrated, the command structure of the IRA had an important decision to make: Did they suspend all operations involving the affected unit, or did they allow the unit to continue its operations while closely monitoring it?

Should the decision be taken to suspend the unit, then an immediate, open and far-reaching inquiry was possible – the 'shotgun' approach. Statements and interviews with a wide cross-section of personnel would be obtained. The preliminary round of interviews would be pleasant and inquisitorial; the second and subsequent interviews would be more aggressive and threatening. The problem with this type of inquiry was that it could be indiscriminate, and personal grudges and political manoeuvring could become entwined with the serious issue of identifying the source of a leak. Interrogations could be resented by innocent volunteers who were subjected to them.

An 'aggressive' interview or interrogation was not a straightforward procedure. The individual or individuals in question needed to be 'arrested', or at least taken to a suitable location where the interrogation could be safely carried out, possibly over an extended period. An urban environment was not ideal for this activity, although in some instances there was no choice. But it was usually possible to sedate an individual and transport him, or her, to a safer area for the more 'hands-on' approach associated with interrogations in remote areas such as parts of south Armagh or across the border in the Irish Republic.

Of course, the objective of an interrogation was to obtain a confession. Standard IRA procedure seemed to be that unless an individual made what the interrogators deemed to be a full confession they would not be killed, but it could be hard to tell whether a confession was real or merely the result of a severe physical interrogation.

Many agents made it through IRA interrogations and interviews without admitting their involvement in touting. Some were put through the mill two or three times. Agents' handlers had a responsibility, where the weight of evidence against an agent was overwhelming, to remove that agent from active duty and relocate him or her. However, in the vast majority of cases, the handler was more likely to simply say: 'Don't worry, we will look after you! Get in there and bluff them out.'

If the IRA took the decision not to suspend the suspected unit but to allow it continue as if there was nothing wrong, the circle of knowledge regarding suspicion was kept to a minimum. Thus the task of pinpointing where the unit had been compromised was made easier. The obvious danger in this strategy was the chance that both equipment and manpower could be at risk. Those involved in planning needed to ensure that all pieces of information were placed in compartments, so that if there was a compromise the task of discovering where, when, and by whom it had been committed was made easier.

Experience showed that this approach had a better chance of identifying a leak. Agents and their handlers could become complacent, and it is this human failing which was the best aid to identification for an IRA security unit. The chances of success were thus maximised if the normal routine of a unit were uninterrupted.

One factor that was always present and was very difficult for an IRA investigating team to identify was the compromise of operations by outside agencies through use of electronic means rather than touts – in other words, 'bugs'. When a leading IRA member was targeted by the FRU or other agencies for electronic coverage, and as a result their operation was compromised, those who were directly involved in the operation would obviously come under internal IRA scrutiny. During the questioning of those involved in the failed operation, or by other subtle means such as the planting by external agencies of misinformation especially through police-friendly media, the IRA would be given the impression that the compromise was the result of a tip-off. The IRA would be looking for a tout.

An example is the case of Paddy Flood who was set up by Scappaticci. Flood was an extremely proficient and loyal member of the IRA. Circumstances and information collected suggested to an IRA investigation team that Flood was a tout. Ingram's experience in the FRU tells him that Flood was not an informer; it was also denied by a very experienced ex-RUC Special Branch police officer in the Irish edition of the *Sunday Times*. The IRA scored an own-goal by removing Paddy Flood.

Another instructive incident was the SAS ambush and shooting of eight IRA volunteers outside Loughgall police station, County Armagh, in May 1987. Rumours circulated that a high-level mole within the IRA supplied information on the operation to the British. Much has been made of RUC claims, and some Army claims, that an informer was indeed at work. In reality, however, Ingram can again confirm that the entire SAS operation was planned as the result of electronic devices planted in the home of an IRA member, not one of those volunteers who died. It was as simple as that. Loughgall proved you didn't always need to recruit agents to infiltrate paramilitary units; all that was needed by the security forces was to know who in a certain area was the 'main man' and electronically target him in his car and in his home.

The complexity of the working of the internal security unit and its penetration by other forces is illustrated by accounts from two individuals who had dealings with it: the murdered IRA 'supergrass' Eamon Collins, author of *Killing Rage*, who worked on the Nutting Squad; and Kevin Fulton.

Scappaticci first interviewed Eamon Collins after a mistake was made by an IRA active service unit – an innocent civilian was shot in a bookie's shop in Newry instead of an

RUC Special Branch man. Collins was impressed by Scappaticci's thoroughness and commitment to the republican cause, as well as by his acceptance of the murder as merely a 'regrettable incident'. Collins admired this cold-hearted approach and this admiration was obviously reciprocated, because Collins was later seconded to work for the internal security unit under Scappaticci.

In June 2003 Collins's co-writer Mick McGovern gave us more details of Collins's first meeting with Scappaticci. '"Will you be going down the Damascus Road, Eamon?" Scappaticci had asked Collins.' The IRA interrogator, sitting behind him in the darkened room, wanted to know if Collins, who had just helped murder an innocent Catholic, might turn to God – and perhaps the police – to repent his sins.

McGovern told us:

> 'Eamon told me when we were writing his autobiography, *Killing Rage*, that Scap had a keen interest in keeping up with new police interrogation techniques – IRA members feared the Nutting Squad more than they feared any police or Army unit. Scappaticci had been arrested and detained countless times. He told Eamon that once, after trying the usual interrogation methods, police spent several hours telling him jokes to try and break his composed manner. Scap said some of the jokes had been very funny, and he had had to fight hard not to crack.
>
> 'At first, Eamon respected and admired Scap, although later his view changed. Scap struck him as ruthless, dedicated and methodical, the epitome of the tough guerrilla fighter that Eamon aspired to be. Eamon felt that with more people of Scap's calibre in the ranks, the

IRA could certainly stave off military defeat, if not achieve outright victory. Eamon regarded Scap as someone who acted in the best interest of the republican movement and who did not abuse his power excessively. Although Scap was normally controlled, Eamon knew he had an explosive temper.

'Eamon loathed his immediate superior in the South Down Command, a man nicknamed Hardbap. He regarded him as a blundering incompetent, botching operations and causing unnecessary deaths to civilians and fellow IRA members. He discovered that Scap too loathed Hardbap because of a fight they'd had many years earlier. Some have claimed that this may have been the incident which pushed Scap into the arms of Army intelligence. Eamon heard that one night after a drinking session in Dundalk, Scap mounted the pavement in his car in an attempt to run over Hardbap. Senior IRA commanders had to talk to the two men to prevent the conflict from escalating.

'Eamon respected Scap as someone who, like himself, had a "normal" job on top of his IRA work. He felt that other IRA members, whose freedom fighting was subsidised by dole money, had a far easier life. But, gradually, he grew to distrust Scap, although he never suspected he might be working for the British.'

In his book, Collins recounts how, when he first joined the feared internal security unit in 1984, Scappaticci would regale him with tales of the interrogations and executions of touts. Scappaticci, then second-in-command of the unit, relished and enjoyed debriefing IRA members for hours on end after they had been released from a grilling by the security forces. He tells how Scappaticci and the then chief of the Nutting Squad, John Joe Magee, told him the grisly story of one man who had confessed to being an informer after being told that he was being offered an amnesty. Scappaticci promised the man that he would take him home, instead of telling him that he was going to be shot dead. Scappaticci proudly told Collins that he constantly reassured the man that he was safe, but made him wear a blindfold as they took him on a journey by car. Scappaticci opened the door and let the man step out onto the road. Scappaticci said that 'It was funny watching the bastard stumbling and falling, asking me as he felt his way along railings and walls, "Is this my house now?" And I'd say not yet, walk on some more.' John Joe finished the story saying 'and then you [Scappaticci] shot the fucker in the back of the head!' Collins spent many hours working alongside Scappaticci – vetting new recruits, debriefing IRA members, conducting courts martial and hunting for suspected informers.

Mick McGovern explained Eamon's growing disillusionment: 'In a key confrontation, Scap failed to speak up for him. Eamon then realised that to Scap, everyone was expendable. Scap's treatment of Eamon intensified a process of disillusionment that had started years earlier. After more than six years in the IRA, with at least five murders on his conscience, Eamon cracked under interrogation in police custody after his arrest for the mortar attack on Newry police station which killed nine police officers. He became a supergrass, telling the police everything he knew, causing huge damage to the IRA and leading to scores of arrests. But in court Eamon withdrew his statements and walked free from Court A, this time for a "debriefing".

'He knew they wanted to kill him, but the IRA had given him a public amnesty and, for practical purposes, could not go back on its word. Eamon waited nervously in an IRA safe house in Dundalk for Scap's arrival. The head of the Nutting Squad came without Scap. He told Eamon that Scap had decided against coming, because he was not sure that he would have been able to control himself. As far as I know, Eamon, who was murdered in January 2000, never saw Scap again.'

※ ※ ※

Former FRU and Branch agent, Kevin Fulton, was a south Down IRA volunteer who worked for the security forces over a long period along the border. Fulton was the agent who called his police handler three days before the Omagh bomb atrocity of August 1998 to tell him that he had met Mooch Blair, a dissident, and that Blair had fertiliser dust on his clothing. This, for an experienced paramilitary like Fulton, was evidence of a bomb being made. Fulton knew, too, that if it had been made that day it would be moved to its target in the following five to seven days.

Fulton told us that he believed his days were numbered when Freddie Scappaticci pulled him in for questioning after a failed IRA operation. In the early hours of 10 February 1994, Gerry Adams's cousin, David Adams, along with Robert Crawford and Paul Stitt, were arrested in the Belmont area of east Belfast as they prepared to kill top RUC officer Derek Martindale – they were later convicted of attempted murder. Adams was beaten so badly during the arrest that he later won £30,000 in compensation. The IRA launched an inquiry. Fulton was suspected of being the informer who compromised the operation. Fulton later made a statement to the RUC. This is what he said:

'It was early 1994 and two Provos ... asked me to get the IRA a mobile phone. They wanted a basher – that is, a mobile phone with the bill going to someone else. My handlers from MI5, Army and RUC Special Branch told me to go ahead and get one. I tried for one week but was unable to get one. [X] from the RUC told me to get one on contract and give it to the IRA and they – my handlers – would look after the bill. So I got a mobile phone in the name of a family member without them knowing, and gave the phone to my handlers. They returned it to me the next day and told me to give it to the IRA.

'After a few days it became clear that things were hotting up. [One Provo] had called me to Belfast to meet him. He told me that the previous night a unit had been moving some gear and crashed the car. He said we needed to replace the car as they had borrowed it from a supporter; I told him I would have a look around. On my way home to Newry I called my handlers and set up a meeting. They told me to go ahead with the car. All they wanted was the make, registration and colour, and the time and place of delivery. When I got the car I gave them all the details that were requested and delivered the vehicle. Over the next few days all was quiet with [that particular Provo]. My handlers kept in touch by phone and by pager. Then a few days later I went down to Belfast and as I turned into [his] street I could see a large number of Army and RUC outside his house. I drove past. There was no doubt they were raiding his house.

'I called my handlers and told them what was going on. They told me to sit tight, and they would call me back later. It was 11.30am when I got the call to go for a meeting. When I arrived I parked my car and waited for the all-clear to move to the van [that my handlers used]. When the nod came I moved to the side door of the Toyota and got in. We then went to the safe house and had a meeting where they told me of the murder bid on Derek Martindale in east Belfast. They told me that they had caught the whole team of IRA men on the job. Then came the bad news. The mobile phone used on the job was the one I supplied and the getaway car was also the car I supplied.

'My handlers told me not to worry, they had everything under control. Then they told me that the family member in whose name I got the mobile phone had been arrested that morning, and that the police were now raiding my home in Newry. They told me that the police were looking to arrest me. They told me to stay in the safe house for that day until they sorted things out. It was decided by my handlers that I would be arrested the next day. I was briefed on what was going to happen next. I was to be arrested and I would be taken to a Belfast holding centre. I was told to say nothing to the police, as they had no idea I was an agent, and that my handlers would keep an eye on everything that was going on.

'I was arrested the next day and taken to Castlereagh holding centre in Belfast, for my first interview. The two detectives sat down and looked at me, then one of them said: "Who the f*** do you work for?" I just sat there as I had been told to. "Who the f*** do you work for?" Again I just sat there. The other cop then said: "We need to know who you are working for, because everything is pointing to you." Again I sat there and said nothing. They said they weren't going to bother to ask me anything as they knew I was working for someone. They said: "If we can work it out, so can the Provos." Five days after the arrests, I was released along with my family member and went home. The next day I was contacted by the Provos in Belfast. They wanted me to come down to the city to talk to the security section – Scap.

'They told me to bring my family member with me. I protested that this person knew nothing about anything. I was then told if I didn't bring this person, "We will send a team down and f***ing drag them here." I called my handlers and told them that I had to go to Unity Flats to meet with the security team. They told me to report what happened and said they were going to keep an eye on things. I saw Scap in the hall on the way in. When we got there I was split up from my family member and taken into a dark room. I was told to sit down and face the wall. Then someone put a blindfold over my eyes. I could hear the sounds of feet on the floor and a chair being moved. A voice said: "Well, Kevin, I want to ask you about the operation, all you know about it and any help you gave. You know you are under arrest and that we are the IRA security unit." I knew only too well what trouble I was in if I made any mistake. My only worry was for my family member who knew nothing, not even who I was really working for. Having worked with the security unit in Dundalk, with John Joe Magee and Scap, I knew the score. If the suspect makes a confession he is finished, dead, down the hole. I didn't need to be reminded. I also knew who I was dealing with. It was Scap, second to big John Joe. Anybody who was anybody knew the voice of Freddie Scappaticci.

'The questions started. "Tell me, Kevin, what did you know about the op and what did [X] ask you to do?" I gave my answers, which was easy to do. I knew nothing about the op and all I did was supply the phone and the car. Then Scap asked about my arrest and how the questions went in Castlereagh. This went on for hours. Scap did this. He repeated questions over and over again and looked for the slightest difference in any answers so that he could pick on them. I knew this was a big investigation because Adams was a top Ra man and, because of his relationship to Gerry Adams, the movement would want answers. I kept giving the same answers, telling myself that I could bluff it. Then I was told that I could go home but I would have to come back two days later.

'That night on the way home my family member told me how scared he was. I felt so bad that this job that I was doing had now touched the ones that I loved. This family member was also told to come back at the same time as me. This was starting to hurt me so much, but there was nothing I could do to stop it. The next day I phoned my handlers. They told me to meet them that evening. I told them what had happened. They kept saying don't worry about it, we are watching, we will know if things go wrong, don't worry. I told them that I was not happy about members of my family being arrested by the police and then by the IRA – but they kept telling me it was good for my cover. They told me not to worry about my next meeting with the IRA, that they were fully aware of things.

'The next day I travelled to Belfast with my family member. When we got to Unity Flats we were taken to separate rooms. I was again told to face the wall. This time there was no blindfold. Already I started to feel better. It was the same questions as before, then the questions changed to ops from the Newry area. I knew they were looking more deeply, maybe into my whole career. I could feel the blood drain from me. There was a five-minute break, then a new interrogator came in. I knew this man also. Again more questions, this went on for about two hours. Then he said that I could go home, but I would have to meet Scap in two days' time. I agreed. It was an offer you couldn't refuse.

'On the way home my family member was crying and shaking with fear. I could never forgive myself or my handlers for what they had done. My relation said he had been told that he did not have to return to the IRA for questioning. From that moment I knew I was for the high jump because although my relative was told he didn't have to be there, I got a different message. Scap definitely wanted to talk to me. When I got home I called in to my handlers and told them what had happened. They set up a meeting for the next day.

'At the meeting, in a safe house in Dromore, we talked about what had taken place the night before and how I was not happy about having to meet Scap the next day. But again and again they kept on saying, "You will be okay," "We are watching what is going on, you are okay." I knew in my own heart that everything was not okay. I knew from first-hand experience what would be going on behind the scenes in Belfast. There was a witch hunt on and I was the witch. I told my handlers that I wanted [to be] pulled out, as had been agreed many times in the past. But they kept on saying to go ahead with the third meeting, that I would be okay. It was all right for them to say that. They would not be tied up like a turkey ready for the oven. Again and again I told them I wanted out. I reminded them of the agreement: If I felt I was compromised they would pull me out. This was the last straw. I knew I was f***ed by my own side too – the Army, MI5 and Special Branch were also ready to shaft me. That's what some of them do to agents when they no longer need them. They knew that I knew. Because I had caught them out before, I knew I had reached the end.

'I had never felt so f***ed over in my life. Everything the IRA had been telling suspect touts was right. The system will use you and spit you out. I never believed it, but now it looked true. It is the duty of all of us to save life if we can. But one must ask, if I save that life by going to the police, and by doing so I am compromised, will the police do everything they can to save my life? Over the years I have learned a lot about some of my former handlers, and some of the agents they handled. A number of them are dead. Murdered. But I have worked with some good police officers in the RUC. I never did go back to see Scap. I left the country and lay low for a while. I knew that if I had gone to that meeting I was a dead man. Scap had sentenced me to death and I had escaped by the skin of me teeth. When I came back Scap was no longer on the scene, thank God.'

Kevin Fulton was lucky. Others were not so lucky.

Chapter 6

Murders in the Republic and Northern Ireland

Harkin/Ingram

Tom Oliver

It wasn't easy writing the story of Tom Oliver when I revisited the story of his death after the exposure of Scappaticci. I knew he had left behind a widow and seven children and any investigation would reopen old wounds. But I believed, and I still believe, the whole truth about what happened to Tom Oliver must be made public. He was sacrificed to save Freddie Scappaticci and questions must be asked about how British agents were allowed to murder citizens of the Irish Republic. After I wrote my first article, a relative of Oliver's rang me to complain and to seek more details. I was unable to help at the time because of legal restrictions. I apologised for the hurt I had caused. I had got no pleasure out of it.

Let's make no mistake about it: the Force Research Unit and other intelligence agencies did not recognise the border that divides Ireland. Military intelligence officers sometimes travelled the length and breadth of the country, checking weapons dumps and recruiting agents. Ingram personally handled quite a few agents in the south over many years – in fact, about a quarter of all agents were from the Republic. Several members of the Garda Síochána worked for the intelligence community over many years and each of them provided valuable information, for, despite what the politicians said publicly, on-the-ground cooperation between the security forces of both states was virtually non-existent, whatever happened at higher levels. In reality, for the FRU the only source of information for the British on southern activity was that supplied by agents.

One Garda officer was recruited whilst in the Republic and became a top agent for the security services. Because of his rank and position he was able to provide detailed information about on-the-run IRA members (OTRs) as well as activists based in the Republic. His motivation was simple – he was anti-IRA, and didn't feel his side were doing enough about them. The money helped too; a Garda salary was nothing to write home about and a few hundred pounds in sterling every month helped this officer take his family abroad on foreign holidays and change his car when he needed to.

Many FRU operations took place in the Republic, but one in particular would cause ramifications many years later – the murder of Thomas Oliver. Oliver was a thirty-seven-year-old farmer from Riverstown, a father of seven, from the County Louth peninsula of Cooley. Late on Thursday, 18 July 1991, he went to attend a new-born calf on his farm, but never returned home. Unknown to family or friends, Tom Oliver had been leading a bizarre double life as a paid informer for Garda Special Branch. Over the six years prior to his death, his information to police had led to the arrests of at least eight republicans and the recovery of a number of weapons. But Tom Oliver was no surveillance expert. He was not, by any stretch of the imagination, a full-time highly paid agent, but he was an informer with a long track record in dealing severe blows against the IRA.

And his lack of expertise is what led to his death. For the farmer always used the same payphone to call his Special Branch contacts to pass on information. At the same time, the FRU was getting information on the same IRA gangs in south Armagh/north Louth from its agent inside the group, Freddie Scappaticci. The Nutting Squad number two was a well-known republican face in the area, but even more so after Scappaticci became a wanted man in the North as RUC CID officers wanted to question him about the abduction and interrogation of Sandy Lynch, the IRA informer, at a house in west Belfast in January 1990 (*see* Chapter 7).

Just days before his death, Tom Oliver went to the public payphone to make a call to his Garda handler. But this time the booth was bugged. The IRA had placed a voice-activated tape recorder inside. Ingram knows for certain that the IRA volunteer who carried out this job was himself working for the FRU. A five-minute phone call followed that would seal the fate of Oliver. The security forces had to decide whether Oliver would live or die – whether he could be 'sacrificed', but they chose not to alert the Gardaí to the fact that there was a risk to his life. And there were lots of reasons why the British security forces might want Oliver dead: firstly, they feared his information could lead to the arrest of Scappaticci while Scap was working inside the Republic – the last thing they wanted was their best agent spending time in Mountjoy. Secondly, if Scappaticci helped to murder an informer this would increase his standing within the IRA at a time when some were unhappy at his role in the Sandy Lynch case. And thirdly, the less Gardaí knew about the Provisional IRA along the border the better, as far as the FRU was concerned. While the FRU had its men in the Gardaí, so did the IRA, and the FRU was highly suspicious of a number of Garda officers in the Republic and was convinced that it knew the identity of at least one who was working for the IRA.

Oliver's body was found dumped in a field near Belleek, County Armagh, less than forty-eight hours after his abduction. He had been tortured, then shot repeatedly in the head. Scappaticci would tell his handlers later that Oliver had confessed to his work for the Gardaí after the tape of his phone call was played back to him. The father of seven suffered a horrible death at the hands of the Nutting Squad. A relative was later quoted as saying: 'Whoever they were, they thumped him and thumped him to get him to say what they wanted him to say. After the post mortem a priest said it looked like they'd dropped concrete blocks on every bone in his body, but I don't think they did that. They just thumped him senseless till he had no idea where he was or what he was saying. I'll never forget, as long as I live, the screams of his wife and the children when they went to the morgue, or the awful silence of the people who went into the yard outside to wait for them coming out.' The murder caused outrage throughout the Republic, but in particular in Cooley, where thousands of people attended an anti-IRA rally.

The murder split republican families for years to come, as locals turned against the Provisionals, and it sucked support away from the IRA in an area where there had traditionally been a strong support base. Known republicans were being shunned in shops and bars, in a wave of revulsion at the brutal killing. Coincidentally, this is exactly the type of revulsion that frequently led a potential informer into the arms of British intelligence.

Gardaí briefed journalists that Oliver had passed information on to them only once, after accidentally coming across weapons on his land. Republican sources confirm that Oliver had been questioned by the IRA in 1991 and was released unharmed. From Ingram's inside information we can confirm two factors relating to his death: that one British agent facilitated the bugging of the phone and that another, Scappaticci, oversaw the interrogation and murder of Oliver.

In May 2003 – after Scappaticci was exposed – *Guardian* reporter Stuart Miller found that all the old wounds caused by the murder had been reopened. He wrote:

> 'Tom Oliver's name still hangs proudly on the sign overlooking the entrance of the family farm. Up the road, in the Olivers' immaculate bungalow, he is there again, greeting visitors with a gawky smile from a gilt-framed photograph hanging in the entrance hall. He can also be found in many of the other houses dotted along the Cooley peninsula of County Louth, where pictures of him are on prominent display. Almost twelve years after he was abducted and killed by the IRA, Tom Oliver remains an inescapable presence on Cooley, the northeast tip of the Irish Republic. Now, in the wake of the Stakeknife revelations, the Olivers and their community have again been thrown into turmoil over the violent death of the man they knew – or believed they knew – so well. Since his death, Oliver's widow Bridie, their seven children and the majority of their neighbours have coped, in the knowledge that he was a law-abiding

citizen brutally murdered by the Provos on false charges of being an informer. The Stakeknife revelations have forced them to confront two new scenarios: that Oliver's murder was tacitly sanctioned by the British security apparatus to protect the identity of its top agent; and that the affable dairy farmer was indeed a regular paid informer for the Garda Special Branch. "This is torturing the family," said Father John McGrain, the parish priest at the time of the murder, who remains a close friend. "They want to get on with their lives but every so often, something brings it all back to the surface again."

"'All the old bitterness and resentment have been dredged up again," said one prominent local. "It now looks like Tom was more involved than anybody wanted to believe." Stuck in the middle of all this, the shell-shocked Olivers have closed ranks in the hope that the allegations will go away. "The house is going mental at the minute. We are not ready to say anything," said Oliver's son Eugene, now twenty-four. Instead, they have vented their feelings through an angry editorial in the local paper, the *Argus*, which demanded an inquiry into the British Army's role and dismissed the informer claims as spurious. "That is what we think and we are not going to add any more to that," said Mr Oliver. They are not the only ones hoping that the story disappears. Most people in the area, while sympathetic, are unhappy about being forced to relive these events. But it is local republicans who have found the intrusion of the past most uncomfortable. Arthur Morgan, a former IRA prisoner who won the County Louth seat for Sinn Féin in last year's Irish general election, was keen to draw a veil over the episode. "I'm not running scared of these questions but realistically I have to say that I don't know that there is anything to be gained by pulling it up all the time." The best the Olivers can hope for is that they are at least a step closer to finally establishing the truth. Few are optimistic. "It is a very murky world we are dealing with," said Father McGrain. "It is hard to believe that anything good will ever come out of this. The only thing we can say for sure is that Tom Oliver died and he died unjustly."'

Father McGrain is right – Tom Oliver did die unjustly. But the role of FRU agent Scappaticci must be exposed. The Olivers are naturally angry over the murder of a loving father and husband and in the interests of justice and fair play they need to know officially of Tom Oliver's role as an informer and what his motivations were. That would be a better conclusion to this whole sequence of sorry events. The Irish Government must also stop playing lip service to inquiry calls and press the British to confirm or deny – on the record – these alarming allegations. But Taoiseach Bertie Ahern will, as he told the Dáil in early 2003, be given the runaround again.

Frank Hegarty

'Franko was a wonderful man, a typical working class Derry man. Not bright, yet streetwise. A gambler by instinct, undoubtedly the day he agreed to get into the back of the handlers' vehicle whilst out walking his greyhound dog was the biggest gamble of his life. The decision which led to his death was to be a political one, not a military one. I had left Derry at the time, but I was gutted when he died.'
Martin Ingram, former co-handler of Frank Hegarty.

The Irish State undoubtedly benefited from some FRU activities. The Hegarty case, in particular, shows how the intelligence services were prepared to put even British soldiers at risk in order to maintain an agent but, when it was politically expedient, would compromise that same agent.

The murder of Frank Hegarty, 'Agent 3018', has been covered widely in the media, in books and on television. It's an alarming story, but one to which we can now bring new information. I was one of Hegarty's handlers and I knew the man intimately. The body of Frank Hegarty – known as Franko – was found dumped less than a hundred yards inside Northern Ireland, at Cavan Road near Castlederg, County Tyrone, on 25 May 1986. He had been horribly tortured, his arms and legs were tied and his eyes were still taped shut. Scappaticci had been brought in by the IRA GHQ for this one, for this one was special. Hegarty had given up a Libyan arms shipment to the British, just the latest in a series of blows he had dealt to the Provisional IRA during his eight years working for the FRU.

Hegarty worked for military intelligence for seven years. He had been an old informer from the 1970s inside the Official IRA, and was suspected of involvement in the 1974 bombing of Ebrington barracks in Derry by the IRA, which left cleaners John Dunn and Cecilia Byrne dead. He later denied this. When agent Hegarty was reactivated in 1982 and began working for the FRU, his information at first was not very good, but by 1985 he was working inside the IRA's quartermaster department, helping to organise arms shipments. His information would ultimately lead to the biggest IRA arms find on Republic of Ireland soil.

What happened was that when the arms shipment arrived from Libya into the south, part of it was earmarked to be sent immediately north while the rest remained hidden. Hegarty, as quartermaster general (QN) of Northern Command, was the person charged by the IRA with organising the transit hides. Hegarty approached the FRU for help with preparing the hides near the border for those arms before scattering them throughout the north. Intelligence officers travelled into the Republic to do this: in the last week of November 1985 officers visited all the hides and took photographs of the weaponry involved. Those are the weapons that were soon to be given over to the Irish authorities. In a tip-off from the British in January 1986 Gardaí found more than 100 rifles and pistols and 21,000 rounds of ammunition at three different hides in counties Sligo and Roscommon. Crates containing weaponry at Carrowreagh in Roscommon bore the inscription 'Libyan Armed Forces – cartridges for weapons'. The timing of the find was hugely significant. It had been just over three months since the signing of the Anglo-Irish Agreement, in which British prime minister Margaret Thatcher and Irish taoiseach Garret FitzGerald had promised new cooperation in the fight against the IRA. As unionists continued their protest against the accord, this find could not have come at a better time – it was an indicator that benefits would come from the Agreement.

The FRU knew that giving up the first Libyan weapons would point the IRA's Nutting Squad directly at Hegarty, who had been entrusted by the Provisionals' Northern Command with securing them before distribution to IRA units across the North. In an ideal world, the FRU would have allowed the weapons to remain in IRA hands but would have jarked them, then monitored their movements. This way it could prevent future IRA attacks and compromise further hides as the weapons could be tracked.

A similar situation had happened before but at that time Hegarty had been protected. Some time previously a team of military intelligence officers had access to a weapons dump controlled by Hegarty. They could jark the weapons or track them, blowing Hegarty's cover, or leave them and place the lives of soldiers, RUC officers and civilians at risk. Left to their own decision-making, without the influence of major political developments, they chose the latter because to expose Hegarty at a time when he was gaining more respect inside the IRA would risk losing more vital information later. In order to jark weapons they would have had to involve the RUC and Hegarty's security would have been affected. He might not necessarily have been discovered, but his security and therefore his potential as an agent, not just in Derry but within the IRA's Northern Command, would have been compromised. The weapons were taken from their hide in the city cemetery by Hegarty and given to the FRU, whose officers test-fired them, checked their ballistics then simply returned them to the hide. But they decided against bugging the hide or jarking the guns.

On 25 January 1986, two phone calls would change the life of Frank Hegarty. One was from prime minister Margaret Thatcher to the head of MI5, ordering them to pass 3018's (Hegarty's) information to the Irish.

The other was from his handler, telling him he had been compromised, that the Gardaí would lift the weapons the next morning and that he, Frank Hegarty, should get to the new Foyle Bridge for a pick-up by his handlers as soon as

possible. As hundreds of Garda officers and Irish Army personnel moved in to lift the weapons at dawn on Sunday, 26
January, Hegarty was being driven to RAF Aldergrove to
board a flight to England. He would spend the next thirteen
weeks in a series of safe houses in Kent and in Brighton.
Every day he spoke to his mother, and over time he began to
speak to Sinn Féin's Martin McGuinness.

Ingram, who was at this stage back in England at the end
of a tour of duty, spent some time during that period with
Frank Hegarty. 'I looked after him for five days, alongside
another girl on temporary relief. We talked about Derry and
how much he missed it. I asked him if he would return, and
he said he would at some stage. I reported this, of course. He
seemed convinced he could talk his way out of it. He was
resentful of his handler, who, he felt, had done the dirt on
him by letting the weapons be lifted.'

On Friday, 24 April 1986, Frank Hegarty went into a bookie's shop in Brighton and gave his handlers the slip. There is
no doubt that he was lured by a feeling of false security. He
arrived at his mother's house, at Osborne Street in the Rose-
mount area of Derry, in the early hours of the Sunday and
spent five days hiding there. At the request of the IRA he
later signed an affidavit saying he would never give evidence as a supergrass. Agent 3018 believed he was now safe,
and agreed to travel to Donegal for an IRA debriefing. He left
his mother Rose's home on the evening of Wednesday, 21
May 1986. His family, including partner Dorothy Robb,
never saw him again. His brother went to identify his body at
the morgue at Altnagelvin Hospital five days later.

Scappaticci and the Nutting Squad were brought in by the
IRA to carry out the 'debriefing' of Frank Hegarty, who

eventually made a full confession of working for the FRU. Following normal procedure, that confession would have been taped, though it was never sent to the family or made public. In fact, his family continues to insist that Frank Hegarty wasn't a security force agent. But he was – Ingram worked with him in the FRU. In a chilling statement issued within hours of the body being found, the IRA gave details of Hegarty's work for the FRU, even how he'd been recruited while out walking his greyhounds in the Glenowen area of the city. The statement added: 'We have now executed Mr Frank Hegarty. Responsibility for the danger in which he finally placed himself rests not with his handlers or the British government but with the Dublin government, now a partner with Britain in the recruiting of agents and spies.' The statement was a clear reference to the Libyan weapons find four months earlier – the IRA knew the Irish authorities would never have discovered the cache without Britain's help.

Portadown informers – Greg Burns, John Dignam, Aidan Starrs

Gregory Burns, from Portadown, had been sourced by the FRU in 1980 after his application to join the Ulster Defence Regiment was turned down. Because of his disaffection he was a classic target for the FRU, though originally with Official IRA leanings rather than Provisional. The FRU targeted people from the whole spectrum of republicanism, including the INLA. What drove Burns to betray his republican roots can only be guessed at, when you consider that at the time there was overwhelming support in nationalist and republican areas for the hunger strikers. Perhaps it was simply for money. Burns was a willing agent, and began providing valuable information to his handlers, information on every IRA volunteer, Sinn Féin member and hunger-strike sympathiser he knew in the Portadown and Lurgan areas. He quickly gained the trust of those in the upper echelons of the republican movement, and became an assistant to Owen Carron, a former Sinn Féin MP who in 1981 worked as the election agent for Bobby Sands, the IRA hunger striker. Burns's information was, as always, passed on to MI5 and RUC Special Branch. On 11 November 1982, Gregory Burns's information would lead to the death of his own brother.

His brother, Sean Burns, along with Eugene Toman and Gervaise McKerr, three IRA members, were travelling along the Tullyglass Road, near Lurgan, when the RUC Headquarters Mobile Support Unit struck. Officers fired a total of 109 rounds at the men's Ford Escort, claiming afterwards that it had crashed through a checkpoint. It was the first of what became known as the 'shoot-to-kill' fatalities, in which a total of six known paramilitaries – all unarmed – died. The deputy chief constable of Manchester, Sir John Stalker, would later state that his attempts to investigate the killings were hampered by lies and deceit at the highest levels within the RUC. He was eventually removed from the inquiry in controversial circumstances and the subsequent inquest into the deaths of Burns, Toman and McKerr became the longest-running Coroner's Court dispute in British legal history.

The three RUC men charged with the murder of the three IRA men were eventually acquitted by Lord Justice Gibson, who said, 'I wish to make it clear that having heard the Crown case I regard each of the accused as absolutely blameless in this matter. That finding should be put in their record along with my own commendation for their courage and determination in bringing the three deceased men to justice, in this case the final court of justice.' Gibson and his wife were later murdered by the IRA.

Burns was obviously distressed after learning that his brother had been shot dead as a direct result of information he had given to his handlers. He was distraught at the wake and funeral, and in the days and weeks which followed. He went to remonstrate with his handlers, and the encounter almost came to blows, with Burns having to be restrained. He was assured that the FRU had not been aware of the RUC operation, that it thought Sean Burns was just going to be arrested. But Gregory Burns was cracking up under the pressure. The FRU relocated him to Amsterdam, Holland, where he continued to work, providing low-level intelligence on republican activities there. But Burns was unhappy there and later roamed Europe, spending many months in Greece. The FRU continued to pay him.

Burns eventually returned to County Armagh and, despite his guilt over the death of his brother, he rejoined the Portadown IRA and continued providing information for the FRU. One republican who knew him in the late 1980s said: 'Greg had a good deal of sympathy [within the movement] because of his brother and how he died and he drank a lot. In fact he seemed to be out drinking most nights and people just put it down to his loss, that he'd get over it in time. Sometimes his behaviour was excused. It was only after his own death that things became clearer. With hindsight it was clear that Greg, Starrs and Dignam became a law unto themselves in Portadown and Lurgan because they were informers and knew the Brits were never going to touch them.' In fact, all three had begun to terrorise their own communities and were involved in numerous 'homers' – operations for their own benefit, including robberies.

Dignam was seen by the public and the media as Sinn Féin's environment spokesman in Portadown, organising 'green' groups for clean-ups in nationalist areas – abandoned shopping trolleys and empty paint tins dumped in streams made headlines in local newspapers. But Dignam had more hidden roles in County Armagh: he was an IRA volunteer; a small-time hoodlum with an appetite for crooked cash; and he was a tout.

Burns was something of a 'ladies man' and although he had a long-term relationship, he had also secretly begun an affair with Margaret Perry, a civil servant. In early 1991, Burns had an argument with her, one of many. Perry had wanted to settle down with Burns, but she was worried about his involvement with the republican movement and told him so. Burns assured her that he was all right, that he was 'untouchable', eventually admitting that he was an agent for the security forces. What she didn't know was that she had fallen for a man who had betrayed his own brother and would, if it came to it, betray her too.

The increasingly erratic behaviour of Burns, Starrs and Dignam was reported to IRA commanders after the robbery of a snooker club. Starrs was questioned by IRA officers about the incident, but was released, unharmed, after denying any role in it. But Margaret Perry, who by this time, April 1991, had ended her relationship with Burns, knew that the three were involved in the theft. Knowing that Burns was working for one or other branches of the security forces,

Perry was in a position to do damage to him and his friends. Perry's relationship with Burns was to cost her her life, for no-one was going to protect her from the three British agents, not even their masters in the FRU.

Two former soldiers, one Irish and one English, who handled Burns, Dignam and Starrs at the time gave an interview on tape to the *Sunday Herald* about the affair in February 2003, before the story broke on the Stakeknife affair. They confirmed the circumstances of Burns becoming an agent after failing entry to the UDR; they also confirmed that he had supplied the information that had led to his brother's death and they detailed Burns's relationship with Margaret Perry. Their motives for speaking out are not clear, but around this time a number of former FRU men were considering becoming whistleblowers. Some had approached the Stevens Inquiry team. These former handlers were all making the same sort of claims – that officers more senior than themselves allowed agents and informers inside the IRA, who were loyal to Britain, to die. They say that Burns Dignam and Starrs wanted out, to be resettled abroad.

'Burns didn't keep his mouth shut and she [Perry] found out he was working for British intelligence,' one of these ex-FRU officers, whom we shall call 'John', said. 'He tried to convince her he was a double agent the IRA had planted within the Army, but she didn't buy it. In late 1990 or early 1991 Burns contacted [the FRU] and told us the game was up. He said he'd been compromised and he, Starrs and Dignam wanted out. The three expected the FRU to set up a resettlement package – a new home, a new identity, a new job and a sizeable pay-off. Burns's handlers went to a more senior officer and said they needed to get the three of them out quickly. Resettling agents is part of the deal. Who on earth would agree to work as an agent for the Brits inside the IRA, if they knew that if they were rumbled we'd abandon them and let them die? But this senior officer wasn't having any of it. He said it was all Burns's own fault and he should get out of the mess himself. He [Burns] said he should silence Perry. The reason the very senior officer didn't want to resettle them was that it costs a hell of a lot of money and manpower. MI5 have to get involved, the local Special Branch in the location [where] the person is resettled need to watch them. He must have just seen it as too much hassle.

'Burns was horrified and came back saying that if he wasn't pulled out of Northern Ireland, he'd have to kill the girl. The senior officer was told about this and he spoke to Burns's handlers, telling them to let Burns know the FRU could not be threatened. It sealed the fate of Burns, Dignam and Starrs as well as Miss Perry. It was a disgraceful breach of promise. There is no doubt an informer who is in risk of their life is capable of murder – we all knew that. Who wouldn't kill to avoid being tortured and executed by the IRA? These people provided [the FRU] with vital information and we owed them. It was the fault of the senior officer. Murder was now inevitable.'

A plot was hatched by the three informers to kill Perry. Burns checked into a hospital in the Republic of Ireland on 20 June 1991 for a minor operation and told Starrs and Dignam to tell Perry that he wanted to see her. As part of the cover story, they were to tell her that he had to use a hospital in the South as it was too dangerous for such a high-profile republican to be seen at Craigavon Area Hospital. The next day, Starrs offered to give Perry a lift to the hospital to see her boyfriend, but he had murder in mind. Not far from Mullaghmore, County Sligo, he stopped the car and strangled the twenty-six-year-old, before finishing her off by beating her over the head with a spade. He buried her body in a shallow grave in a forest not far from the estate of the late Lord Mountbatten. He returned the next day with Dignam who helped him rebury her.

John, the former FRU officer, continues: 'Burns was informed by his friends she was dead and checked himself out of hospital. He told the FRU the matter had been taken care of, that she was dead. From then on it was a Pontius Pilate job – people like that senior officer washed their hands of any guilt to do with the needless death of this girl. If [he] had done what he was supposed to do – protect the agents working for them – none of these people would have needed to die. Instead, the IRA were able to tape the confessions of these guys and get masses of information about how we operated. It was a nightmare scenario. In a senior officer's eyes, Burns just wasn't important enough to resettle. So we ended up with four unnecessary deaths and the compromising of British Army intelligence officers, which ultimately put soldiers' lives at risk. To this senior officer, it was always a matter of the ends justifying the means. Northern Ireland would have been better off without him – and that's saying something.'

Another former FRU officer confirmed much of this information. He promised the *Sunday Herald* to go public with it, and to go on the record with Sir John Stevens, because he feared a 'whitewash' inquiry into the FRU's activities. This ex-handler, who we shall call 'Duncan', says that ninety-nine percent of FRU operations and activities were within the law and aimed at ending 'terrorism', but that there were some rogue elements and it was these elements he wanted to expose. With the clamour for some sort of truth commission in Northern Ireland, he said he felt that an amnesty for all deaths would be helpful, but only if the full truth emerged and those responsible for deaths were at least brought to book by a commission. Duncan added: 'No matter what happens, senior officers who used loyalists as an extension of the Army to carry out the assassination of Catholics on the one hand, and on the other allowed other agents to take out IRA members or suspected informers, must be disgraced publicly. They must lose their jobs and their pensions, but above all, Britain must never allow this sort of thing to happen again, anywhere.' This was the first time that Army intelligence officers confirmed this scenario – a scenario outlined by the IRA more than a decade before.

Exactly what happened next can only be guessed at. Did someone in the FRU throw Dignam, Burns and Starrs to its agent Freddie Scappaticci? The IRA's Northern Command ordered an inquiry, which would have involved Scappaticci in his role in the internal security unit. Scappaticci would certainly have informed his handlers of the inquiry into Dignam, Burns and Starrs, and they would have known that Scappaticci had been brought in to do the interrogation. This was normal practice.

The IRA's inquiry into what happened to Margaret Perry came after a series of embarrassing articles in the *Sunday*

World, written by journalist Martin O'Hagan, who was later murdered by loyalists. O'Hagan all but named the three IRA men as suspects in the death of Perry, and his information was so accurate that the IRA had to act upon it, though they waited a whole year before doing so. All three men were taken out of active service as the investigation into the snooker club robbery and Miss Perry's disappearance began.

But why had it taken a year for the IRA to act? O'Hagan claimed that the IRA refused to believe his articles, and that only after pressure from grassroots republicans did the IRA leadership decide at last to launch an investigation. Some senior republicans had refused to countenance any involvement in anything dishonourable by Burns because of his family history. O'Hagan also claimed that the IRA deliberately waited until the anniversary of Perry's disappearance, then placed a listening device in a car used by Dignam and Starrs in the hope that they would discuss it. And discuss it they did. Dignam and Starrs were picked up by the IRA and taken to two separate houses in Omeath used by Scappaticci and Magee. Burns was abducted two days later and taken to a third location in north Louth.

Freddie Scappaticci and John Joe Magee spent a week interrogating Burns, Dignam and Starrs. All three were tortured and all three confessed to working for the enemy. All three were sentenced to death. Under the IRA's General Army Orders, the death penalty can only be carried out after the Army Council has received 'written records or other records of the proceedings of the Court'. Dignam knew by this stage that he was going to die, and Scappaticci ordered his blindfold removed so that he could write one last statement, which would be revealed to the world within days. He knew his time was up, that he had just hours left on this earth. A blanket was placed over the father-of-two's head, to protect the identity of his interrogator, and John Dignam wrote his last statement, a letter to his pregnant wife. It read: 'I am writing this letter to apologise for all the pain and heartache I have caused you. I have only a matter of hours to live my life. I only wish I could see you and the kids one last time but as you know it is not possible.'

To record the confessions of informers Scappaticci always used the same procedure. A blanket or coat would be placed over the head of the informer and a microphone or paper and pen passed inside. The informer would be told to read from a statement dictated or written earlier. The signal for the informer to begin reading his statement would be the sound of a saucepan being banged. This noise can be heard on the taped confessions of many alleged informers, especially in Dignam's case and that of estate agent Joe Fenton.

On 30 June 1992, Perry's body was found in its shallow grave after an IRA tip-off to a local priest. Two days later – and twelve days after being detained by their IRA bosses – the mutilated bodies of the three informers were found, dumped at various points along a ten-mile stretch of the border. Burns's body was dumped on the Cullaville Road, near Crossmaglen. Dignam's body was found at Deburren, near Lislea, while Starrs's body was found on the Dundalk Road near Newtownhamilton. Press Association photographer Martin McCullough took pictures of the bodies before police arrived. Each had been stripped naked and shot twice through the head. Cigarettes had been stubbed out on Burns's thigh and there was a poker mark in Starrs's armpit. It was a chilling statement from the IRA to informers. And there was a final insult. Milk crates had been placed over or near each body to make the British Army's recovery operation more difficult, with Army technical officers forced to check each scene meticulously for booby traps.

The killings, the first in Northern Ireland after a quiet period of eight weeks, were widely condemned by politicians in Britain and Ireland, including UK prime minister John Major and Irish taoiseach Albert Reynolds. Major, whose government at the time was in secret contact with the IRA, told the House of Commons that the discovery of the bodies and the admission of responsibility for their deaths by the IRA 'demonstrates yet again the true nature of terrorism'. Seamus Mallon, SDLP MP for Newry and Armagh, said that the killings were 'barbarous' and 'obscene', adding: 'It is a perversion of justice, because these people have decided they are going to act as judge, jury and executioner and have done it in a way that has shocked anyone with any sense of humanity left in them.'

In explaining why the men were killed, the IRA issued an unusually detailed statement to a Belfast journalist, saying that the three men had worked for military intelligence. The statement said that Burns had assisted MI5 since 1979, being paid £200 a month, and had given information to the security forces about the movements of his brother before his death. The IRA also said that all three men were involved in the murder of Margaret Perry.

Taped confessions were posted to relatives of each of the men in April 1993, nine months after their deaths. A year after the men's deaths, BBC journalist Peter Taylor attempted to unravel the complex issues surrounding the deaths of the three IRA informers and Perry. In his ground-breaking documentary, he broadcast the taped confessions of the three men, shining light into the dark and dangerous world of the IRA's internal security unit. It is not clear from the Burns or Starrs tapes whether or not they had been told they were going to die. Republican sources at the time said they had been and had accepted their fate, but it is just as likely they were told they were going to be released. That was one of Freddie Scappaticci's tactics, to assure a suspected informer that the movement might be lenient if they came clean.

In his taped confession Burns gave an account, though far from detailed, of his life as a British agent. He confirmed his application to join the UDR and how, after that application was turned down, he was approached by 'two boys' and asked to work for the enemy. He was motivated politically, leaning more towards the Official IRA than the Provisionals. He also had financial motivations: 'I and the wife had an argument about money,' he said. The 'two boys' asked him to report back on Sinn Féin meetings and hunger strike rallies. 'They said they didn't mind how big or small my reports were.'

Burns continued to work for them right up until Perry's death. He confirmed tipping off his handlers about the operation during which his brother Sean was shot dead by the RUC, and said he confronted his handlers afterwards. 'I asked them what the fuck was going on. They offered me some whiskey and I wouldn't take it.'

In his confession, Burns also claimed that when he tried to quit his work for the FRU he was threatened that he would be set up and end up behind bars. This was not, however, a tactic employed often by the FRU, and it is possible that this statement was an attempt by Burns, like many people on the wrong end of a Scappaticci–Magee investigation, to belittle his own role as an informer. Alternatively, it is possible that he was told to say this for the benefit of the tape, to deter future agents.

The three taped confessions detail robberies and extortion rackets that the men were involved in, all carried out using the IRA's name. The snooker club robbery features heavily in Starrs's confession. He recalls how he had been summoned to Monaghan to answer allegations relating to the incident and was questioned by a senior member of the IRA's Northern Command. Starrs describes how he denied involvement: 'He says, "Just tell me the truth and that's it. It's all over with. It's no big deal." But I was frightened. I'd said no the first time and I stuck to that.' Starrs also makes it clear that Margaret Perry knew about that robbery. 'She was on about the snooker club,' he says. 'I know it's hard to understand but it was just a general personal hate that grew within me. I discussed it with Greg [Burns] and we decided that we'd kill her.' He details how he lured Perry across the border on the pretext of meeting up with Burns. In County Sligo he killed her. 'I put the cord round her neck and strangled her. I ran back down to the car and got the spade which I had in the boot. When I came back up again, she still sort of moved a bit, like, and in the panic I just hit her over the head with the spade twice. Then I dug a hole, dragged her over and buried her.' Starrs then describes how he returned to Portadown, told Dignam of the murder and took him back to Mullaghmore to help erase any forensic evidence from the scene. Starrs' verbal delivery is clearly that of a man reading from a prepared statement. There is no emotion.

In his confession Dignam says of the murder scene: 'I still didn't believe he'd done it until I got there. What I seen was a bit of leather jacket and a bit of denim sticking out of the ground. He found the bit of tape and a beer can. He just proceeded to put more dirt over to try to cover her up more. I just put a bush over where the girl was.' Starrs and Dignam then visited Burns in hospital and told him that Margaret Perry was dead. Burns says he rang his handlers the following day. 'I told them that the girl was dead. My words were: "She's fucking dead. What the hell's going to happen?" I hung up and never contacted my handlers from that.'

Starrs and Dignam claim that they only started to work for the security forces after the RUC arrested them and questioned them about Perry's disappearance. But evidence from their former FRU handlers shows that they both worked for the FRU and also for the Special Branch for a number of years. Perhaps the tapes were made at a time when Scappaticci and/or Magee had offered to let them go in return for a confession. Playing down their roles as informants may have been part of that.

Mary Perry, Margaret's mother, said later that she had no doubt that the reason she searched for her daughter in vain for more than a year was because Burns, Starrs and Dignam were being protected by the intelligence agencies. Her daughter and John Dignam were eventually buried a few feet away from each other in the same graveyard. She said at the time that she could never forgive her daughter's killers, adding: 'I would love to be able to say that I do, but I haven't got the strength to do that. I can't fool God by paying lip service. I just hate them, even though they are dead.'

Chapter 7

'Get Danny Morrison'

Harkin

Danny Morrison and Anto Murray were edgy as they walked towards Carrigart Avenue in the Lenadoon area of west Belfast. It was a cold, damp, dark Sunday evening in January 1990 and Murray had picked up Morrison from his home to take him to a safe house where an informer was being held. But something didn't add up for the Sinn Féin publicity director as they entered the street where the informer was waiting. A couple sitting in a car looked straight at them as they passed. Murray turned to Morrison and said, 'I don't like that. That looks suspicious.' They walked on, reassuring each other that there was nothing to it.

In the car the two undercover Special Branch officers were delighted. Their prey had arrived and they knew they were just seconds away from one of the most dramatic arrests of the Troubles. At 124 Carrigart Avenue, in the spare bedroom of the Martin family, Special Branch agent Alexander 'Sandy' Lynch was being held by jailers from the Provisional IRA. He was the Branch's human bait, being used to lure Morrison to the house. As Morrison walked up the pathway to the house he thought about the car again and said to Murray, 'I still don't like that [the car].' As he walked through the outer front door, the Branch detectives gave the order for the raiding party to descend on the area.

Danny Morrison had just stepped through the vestibule door and into the hallway when he heard the distinctive noise of the diesel engine British Army Land Rovers outside. Murray ran halfway up the stairs and looked out a hallway window before shouting, 'The f***ing cops, they're outside.' For a moment, Morrison considered stepping back out through the front door and onto the street, but in those few seconds he knew the situation for him was grave. He went out through the living room, avoiding conversation or eye contact with people sitting there, and headed straight for the back door and opened it. He could see soldiers arriving at the rear of the house. One of the soldiers, Private Cairns, shouted 'halt' and Morrison bolted over a fence and opened the first door he found. It was the rear entrance of the house next door, number 126.

It was ten minutes past five in the evening as Morrison, who had donned a cap and gloves earlier to protect him from the bitter cold, walked into the living room of number 126. In the corner was Mrs Mary Daly, a pensioner in poor health, lying on a settee. Sitting beside her were her daughter Jacqueline and her son James. Her four grandchildren were playing beside them. Morrison told them: 'Don't panic, if anyone comes to the house tell them I'm just visiting.' The Sinn Féin publicity director did not know what to do but he did know that, with an informer next door and the house being raided, it was only a matter of time before the police would arrive looking for him. As James Daly took the four children upstairs, Morrison removed his cap, opened the glass door of the Parkray fire and threw it inside. For the next twenty-five minutes he made small talk with the Dalys, spending most of that time in the kitchen so as not to cause any further distress to the elderly lady in the living room.

At 5.35pm Constable Barklie and Constable Power entered the house and saw Morrison standing in the middle of the living room drinking from a glass of water. The householder was asked if she knew Morrison and she said 'no'. The Sinn Féin man claimed that he did know them, and was just visiting. A soldier was brought in and he said he had seen a 'bald man' leaving next door and going into No. 126. As Morrison had been wearing a cap – now burning in the grate of the Parkray fire – this identification evidence was flawed. But at 6.08pm Danny Morrison was arrested.

Just minutes later at RUC headquarters at Knock, in east Belfast, a phone call was made to a journalist. 'We've got Danny Morrison on a kidnap rap. Put it out. He was in a house where an informer was being held and we've lifted the entire team.' They hadn't. Sandy Lynch's chief interrogator at Carrigart Avenue, Freddie Scappaticci, was already in Dundalk, County Louth, and well outside the jurisdiction as news of the arrests broke that Sunday evening. He had just taken part in his most daring operation yet for British military intelligence. Now he would have to prepare his defence for the IRA, and this time and for the first time his internal security department wouldn't be asking the questions.

Nine weeks earlier, on 9 November, Alexander 'Sandy' Lynch, RUC Special Branch agent and IRA volunteer, had been ordered to attend a meeting with Freddie Scappaticci. It was a 'friendly' interview at a safe house in north Belfast. An IRA operation may have been compromised and Scappaticci had been brought in to debrief Lynch's unit to see what may have gone wrong. The IRA at the time had two ways of dealing with possible informers in their ranks – one was abduction and interrogation once suspicion had fallen on a particular volunteer; the other was debriefings of entire active service units when those suspicions couldn't be pinned down to a specific volunteer. No security measures had been put in place by Scappaticci in this instance – each of the volunteers he questioned spoke directly to him and saw his face. They were all allowed to leave the house in the republican New Lodge district but were each warned to be 'careful'. Lynch's wife had just had a miscarriage and he was uneasy, but he managed to get through his 'chat'. Scappaticci was biding his time. He had other plans for Sandy Lynch, plans not drawn up by the Army Council or the Internal Security Unit, but by his handlers in the FRU and officers of RUC Special Branch.

On Tuesday, 2 January 1990, Sandy Lynch was called to an urgent meeting with his Special Branch handlers at a car park in Holywood, County Down, about six miles from Belfast city centre. He was told that there were new suspicions about him inside the IRA and that he was going to be 'picked up' that Friday afternoon for questioning. His handlers told him not to worry, that as long as he didn't admit to anything, the IRA would stick to their rules and he would be released. The Special Branch were relying on good information. He had survived questioning in December and he would do so again, and in any event the security forces would be keeping an eye on him throughout.

The Branch officers did indeed have reliable information, passed on by the FRU. Scappaticci had told them of plans to detain and interrogate Lynch that Friday. A few years earlier the IRA Army Council had come to a new policy decision. They were worried that the internal security department had been overzealous in a number of informer killings. In fact there had been complaints from across the North from grass-roots republicans that a number of innocent people may have died. The new policy was that no final decision on what should be done to any alleged informer could be made without a representative of the Army Council present, though we understand this still did not always happen. The FRU knew this thanks to Scappaticci, and RUC Special Branch also knew this because of intelligence shared through MI5.

Scappaticci was to inform his handlers of the address where Lynch was to be detained as soon as he knew. Special Branch would then lie in wait for the arrival of the Army Council member or representative. They couldn't be absolutely certain that such a senior IRA member would arrive, but it was a worthwhile gamble. They wanted Sinn Féin publicity director Danny Morrison. The arrest of such a high-profile figure would deal a severe blow to the republican movement and boost morale among members of the security forces.

Lynch was at home in Magherafelt, County Derry, on the afternoon of Friday, 5 January, three days after his meeting with his handlers, when he got the phone call he'd been expecting. He was to go to a house in the New Lodge district of north Belfast at 6.30pm for a meeting of the intelligence-gathering unit, the unit he had infiltrated for the RUC. Inside the house he met Kevin Mulgrew, the head of that unit, and Sean Maguire, Mulgrew's deputy. Lynch knew that he was going to be 'arrested', and his suspicions were confirmed when he was told by Mulgrew that he and Maguire would be using a car loaned from a sympathiser, rather than Lynch's own car, to check out a drug dealer's house in Upper Dunmurry Lane on the outskirts of west Belfast. Lynch was to drive.

When the two IRA members arrived in Upper Dunmurry Lane a few minutes later, Maguire got out to check out the house, leaving Lynch alone in the car for several minutes. This was a clear breach of security rules when luring a suspected informer into the hands of the security unit. However, Lynch made no effort to escape, even though he knew he was going to be interrogated later that day. Maguire then told Lynch they were going to another meeting, this time in Lenadoon, a staunchly republican area of west Belfast.

When they got to the house at Carrigart Avenue, Lynch followed Maguire up the stairs. He was followed by another man. Lynch was pushed down onto a bed as he heard the words 'IRA security'. It was now 7pm.

At about the same time, Freddie Scappaticci called one of his handlers, who we will call 'David', working in the special unit set up solely to handle their best agent. The 'Rat Hole', a self-contained building dedicated to Stakeknife, was located away from prying eyes in Thiepval Barracks, the British Army's headquarters in Northern Ireland. Stakeknife told David that Lynch had indeed been 'arrested' by the IRA, and gave him the address where he was being held. He assured his handlers that he would be playing a personal role in the interrogation, but would be out of the house by teatime on Saturday. After that it was over to the Force Research Unit and RUC Special Branch.

Sandy Lynch was placed face-down on a bed in a darkened rear upstairs bedroom at number 124, his eyes blindfolded with cotton wool and bandages and his hands tied behind his back. He was stripped naked and his clothes were searched. There was panic in the room a few seconds later when a bug detecting device went off, but the IRA unit could find no bugging devices on Lynch or in the room. Lynch said later, 'I heard a voice, which I believed to be Scappaticci. He was swearing and saying the antibugging device was going haywire.' Scappaticci said the equipment must have been faulty as they could find no device. Was he himself wearing a bugging device or was the anti-bugging device itself, which Scappaticci had brought to the house, bugged? Or was someone else in the room wearing one? Perhaps Scappaticci was correct, that the device was faulty. Whatever the reason, the operation should have been aborted at that stage and Lynch should have been moved to another location. For it to continue was 'madness', according to one senior republican source. But continue it did.

Scappaticci went into another room, and a man from Northern Command began the questioning. It continued for more than an hour as Lynch continued to deny he was a security force informer. Then Scappaticci arrived back in the room. We do not believe that Lynch knew Scappaticci was an informer at this stage, though he would find out later.

We believe he did this because he was expecting to be rescued; there was no point in holding out or being tortured or being brave when he was being 'watched'. At the subsequent trial, Lord Chief Justice Sir Brian Hutton described what happened next:

'The questioning by the first two men ended when the man from Northern Command said that they were going to eat and have a bit of a kip and that another team would take over. The first team stopped talking to him [Lynch] and he heard a voice which he recognised as the voice of Scappaticci. The voice asked, "Do you know who I am, Sandy?" He replied, "Yes." Scappaticci said that it did not really matter and that he did not give two fucks because where he [Lynch] was going he would not be able to tell anybody. Scappaticci referred to a meeting before Christmas when he [Lynch] had been debriefed by the security department. He [Scappaticci] said he [Lynch] knew who he was. The same person [Scappaticci] had come up the stairs behind him when he first came into the house.

'Scappaticci had his elbow on his shoulder and his chin on the top of Lynch's head. Scappaticci was very aggressive and foul-mouthed. Scappaticci said he did not like talking to him the way he was talking. He said that if he did not admit to being a tout he would get a jab up the arse and wake up in south Armagh. He would then talk to him the way he wanted to talk to him. He said he would wake upside down in a cattle shed. It did not matter if he screamed, as no one would be around to hear his screaming. Scappaticci asked him how his wife was feeling; he knew she had had a miscarriage before Christmas. He asked him if his wife was in a fit of depression and he replied "yes". Scappaticci asked how she would feel having to come down to identify him with no face, because he [Scappaticci] would make sure he had no face. Scappaticci tapped him a few times on the back of the head, and said that he would get it right there, "like that cunt Fenton". He said his [Fenton's] family could not identify him; he could only be identified by his jewellery.

Scappaticci said he [Lynch] would end up the same way.

'Scappaticci said that he had all the operations that he [Lynch] was ever involved in with the IRA. They knew exactly what he had touted on, but they wanted him to admit it. Scappaticci went into details of all the jobs and how long they said that he [Lynch] was working for the police. He [Lynch] kept denying what was being said.

'Most of the interviewing lasted about an hour. He [Lynch] did not really know about time. He was frightened. He knew he was not going out of the house. He knew they were not making idle threats and he knew he would end up dead. Scappaticci told him that another team were coming in and that they [Scappaticci's team] were going away to get a kip.

'The other team took over again. Scappaticci did not go away, and kept butting in. He said he was taking a very personal interest and wanted to be there when he [Lynch] was taken out. The further questioning from the first team centred around financial matters. They asked about his car, how much was on hire purchase and how much insurance he paid, and things like that. He was asked about a scanner which he had bought. A scanner is a radio for listening to police on the air waves. They said that they believed that he had been handed the scanner by police to give to the unit and that it was bugged. It was suggested to him that he had a clear passage from the police to travel from his home to Belfast.

'He [Lynch] was still denying everything they were saying. At one stage the man from Northern Command said that he alone had the power to grant him an amnesty, but the offer would only last for an hour. He kept telling him [Lynch] not to be sitting there feeling

Above: After training, successful FRU candidates would join together in a passing out parade. This picture shows the new recruits in 1981, including Martin Ingram.
Below: It was important for team-building for FRU officers to socialise together, and they did this often. Here FRU officers meet for a black-tie dinner to say goodbye to a senior officer who is leaving the unit. This was called 'the dining out'.

Above: Ingram with colleagues at a bar solely used by FRU officers, at St Angelo military base in Fermanagh in the late 1980s. FRU members would meet regularly for a drink and to discuss ongoing cases.

Below: Ingram with his FRU colleagues before going on duty in civilian clothes.

Left top and middle: In order to meet agents, the FRU needed safe houses in the community. Pictured are two such debriefing centres (DBCs) in Fermanagh. These two houses were used in the 1980s, and are no longer used or owned by the military.

Bottom: Ingram (sitting down) with two other FRU officers on a military exercise at Ballykinlar Army base, County Down, in 1988.

Above left: A picture of Brian Nelson released to the press by the UDA after his arrest by the Stevens Inquiry. Above right: Pat Finucane, the Belfast solicitor murdered at his home in February 1989. Below left: Francisco Notorantonio was sixty-six when he was shot dead by the UDA/UFF at his west Belfast home in October 1987. Below right: Notorantonio's daughter Charlotte wants an inquiry held into his death.

Above: Gerry Adams carries the coffin of Brendan Ruby Davison in 1987,
as Freddie Scappaticci (circled) walks behind.
Below left: Scappaticci, in a police picture taken in 1974.
Below right: Scappaticci during his now-infamous TV appearance in May 2003,
when he denied being an informer.

Above left: Farmer Tom Oliver, an informer for Garda Special Branch, was murdered by the IRA's internal security unit.
Above right: Margaret Perry, who was brutally murdered in a plot involving **(left)** Gregory Burns, **(bottom left)** John Dignam and **(bottom right)** Aidan Starrs.

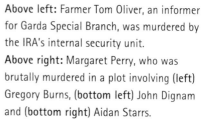

Above: Garret Fitzgerald and Margaret Thatcher at the signing of the Anglo-Irish Agreement in November 1985.

Below: The body of John Dignam lies near a border road shortly after his interrogation and murder by the IRA's internal security unit. A plastic milk crate was placed on the body, so that security forces would think it was booby trapped.

PICTURE: MARTIN MCCULLOUGH.

Above: Danny Morrison, publicity director of Sinn Féin, was so succcessful that the British government banned him and his colleagues from the airwaves. Since leaving prison he has become involved in community issues and is now a regular contributor to newspapers including the *Irish Examiner*. He plans to appeal his conviction.

Below left: Freddie Scappaticci goes back into his house in Andersonstown, moments after speaking to Greg Harkin on 10 May 2003.

Below right: Sir John Stevens hands over his interim report to Hugh Orde, Chief Constable of the PSNI, in April 2003. Orde was in charge of the day-to-day running of the Stevens Inquiry until he left to head the PSNI.

sorry for himself. The man from Northern Command said that he was his salvation and if he admitted to him there would be a bit of leniency. After an hour he would be taken somewhere else when he admitted to being an informer.

'At one stage the man from Northern Command put a scenario to him which he believed was when and how he [Lynch] started working for the police. He suggested it was from the time he was taken to Castlereagh during the last year and he had been working for them for about roughly eighteen months. He [the man from Northern Command] said that he [Lynch] had been arrested in relation to something in south Derry and he knew that he [Lynch] had been working under duress from the police and not of his own free will, and this would go well for leniency.

'He [Lynch] was very agitated and frightened. He knew that if he admitted to being an informer he would be shot dead and that if he did not admit to being an informer he would be shot dead. He was hysterical. A couple of times he was brought water, but he could not drink it and wet his lips. He [Lynch] was asked to name the names of the police, and their addresses and where he met them. At this stage Lynch had made no admissions to them.

'The man from Northern Command said that there were five minutes of the amnesty left and after that he would wash his hands of him. He [Lynch] said that if he admitted to being an informer he would be killed. The man from Northern Command said that that was not necessarily the truth and that it was his [Lynch's] only salvation. The man from Northern Command put the scenario to him [Lynch] and he [Lynch] admitted to him he was right in what he said. The man from Northern Command asked him when he had begun to act as an informer and he said it was what he [the man from Northern Command] said, when he [Lynch] was taken into Castlereagh. He asked him for names of the police and where they met and the type of cars they drove and things like that. He [Lynch] told him the first names of police, which was all he knew, he said that the cars and meeting places were changed regularly. The man from Northern Command asked him how much money he received and he asked him what his codename was and he told him.

'The man from Northern Command said that he [Lynch] would have to make a written statement. He said the statement would go across to the leadership along with the recommendation as to what to do. He said he would make a good recommendation and the other fellows would be fair. Lynch agreed to make a written statement. He thought this was about the early hours of Saturday morning. Lynch was told the blindfold was going to be taken off and his hands untied to write the statement. A coat was put over his head. When the blindfold was taken off his eyes were watering and very irritated. He was told to open the coat and he saw a sheet of paper resting on the newspaper. Scappaticci was giving the instructions at this time. Scappaticci told him to write the statement, keeping it very vague. They had all the details and he was not to go into detail. Scappaticci told him to start with his name and address and that he was making a statement of his own free will. He was then to write that he was an informer, the jobs he had informed on, the money he had received, and if he wanted at the end of the statement to put in a plea for leniency. He was told to admit that what he had done was wrong but it would be a greater wrong to kill him, and his family would suffer. He was told to write at the bottom that he made the statement of his own free will.

'Lynch made this statement and signed it. He was told to close the coat over his head and he was allowed to sit with the blindfold off and his hands untied. He [Lynch] was told that the statement and recommendation and everything relating to the case would go over to the leadership, who would decide what to do. He was told not to be worrying about it and that the IRA were not as hard-hearted as everyone thought. He was told that his statement would probably mean he would have to go to a press conference and live outside the country. It would have been Saturday morning some time when he made the admissions; he was not clear about the times.

'The next event was that he heard someone coming up the stairs and a lot of scurrying and whispering at the door. Scappaticci said to him that the cunts across the road were not satisfied with the written statement and they said that they wanted to make a tape of the confession. A tape would be made and brought across for them to hear his [Lynch's] voice. His hands were still untied and the bandage and cotton wool were off; he was holding the coat tight over his head. There was a bit of scurrying and a microphone was passed under his right arm. Scappaticci told him to open the coat and to read the statement. The statement was on a chair in front of him and he was told to read the document into the tape. The tape was then rewound and played, but it had missed the first part of the statement. He was told to read the statement again, which he did. The tape was then played back and Scappaticci said that it was okay.'

During a preliminary inquiry in the Lynch case, the RUC informer denied that he had ever been involved in the shooting of a man in County Down in 1987. Defence lawyers challenged Lynch that if it could be proven that he was lying, all his evidence would be tainted. Lynch agreed.

This, for the first time, is evidence that Lynch was indeed lying. In May 1991, on the day Danny Morrison and the others were arrested, Peter Duggan was in a flat in London watching the teatime ITN news. The fact of Morrison's conviction and prison sentence was the big story of the day; the man who had been publicity director for Sinn Féin had been found 'guilty'. A photograph of Sandy Lynch appeared on screen and Peter Duggan recognised it. It was the man who had shot him four years earlier at a flat in Downpatrick. The next morning he called Morrison's lawyers and on 21 May 1991, at the Irish Club in Eaton Square, Peter Duggan gave a statement.

That statement, if true, would be devastating for the security forces and for any subsequent Court of Appeal hearing. It read:

'I am now twenty-four years old and left Northern Ireland in 1988 having given evidence in the trial of Mary Clinton and Bernadette Armstrong who were both charged with my false imprisonment in January of that year. I do not wish to disclose where I now live but I have not returned to Northern Ireland since the trial apart from one brief visit for a medical appointment in

Dundonald Hospital. I was born in Belfast ... in 1967 ... I attended Violet Hill College in Newry as a boarder for one year after primary school but left after the year to go to St Malachy's in Castlewellan. I was asked to leave there when I was fifteen years old prior to doing my exams. Although I had a home tutor I sat no exams at all and obtained no qualifications.

'I did not and still do not get along very well with my family and left to travel Europe when aged sixteen. I travelled for a number of years doing any kind of work at all. I now speak passable French. I would have frequently returned home for short periods but would not have stayed very long. I usually didn't work when in Ireland. I occasionally stayed at home in Maghera with my mother, but usually with friends. I was friendly with William Mulhall, who owned an amusement arcade in Downpatrick. I frequently lived above the arcade and helped him out in the running of his business.

'I myself have an extensive criminal record – driving offences, several convictions for deception, VAT fraud but nothing for violence or anything of a terrorist nature. Prior to Christmas 1987 I had been working in Europe for some time and returned about a week before Christmas. I stayed with my mother but would have visited Mulhall with whom I was quite friendly as I have already said. I personally have no and had no terrorist links but would have been aware who was who in and around Downpatrick.

'Earlier in 1987 when I was living in Downpatrick above the amusement arcade I had been the victim of an attack. Firstly the flat was vandalised when I was not there and later that day I was attacked and beaten by three men. I spent the night in Downpatrick Hospital suffering from cuts and bruises. The people who attacked me were [three men] – I believe they were also responsible for vandalising the flat. Sean Braniff was also present when I was being beaten up. All these people would have been known INLA activists in that area.

'I did not know these people well and am not certain why they did this. I think it may have been connected to the theft of money from a friend of mine by these people. I had witnessed [two of the men] steal the money from her in the arcade about a week earlier. They grabbed about £80 from her – one held her and the other took the money out of her hand. Neither she nor I reported this matter to the police but I did tell someone (whom I know to be connected to the Provos). Somehow the police also found out about this incident and [the two men] were interviewed about it. I think that they thought that I told the police and decided to wreck the flat and beat me up. This latter incident I did report to the police.

'Some weeks after this I left for Europe again. I cannot remember exactly when. Anyway, on New Year's Eve 1987 I was in Mulhall's arcade when Mary Clinton came in. We had never met before but were introduced. She issued a general invitation to a party in the Model Farm estate that night. Mulhall decided not to go but I decided to go anyway. I did not know who Mary Clinton was and that her husband was a well known INLA man in the district. I went to the party and was introduced to Bernie Armstrong in whose house the party was taking place. I realised during the party that there were a number of INLA people present. There were only about ten people there altogether.

'I got along well with Bernie and Mary. During the

following week or so I saw quite a bit of them. They contacted me a few times and I saw them both quite a lot at Bernie's house. I actually packed my things and went to stay in Bernie's for a while before leaving the country again, which I intended to do.

'I had been staying at Bernie's a couple of days when [I was] invited over to Clinton's for coffee. I think this was a Wednesday evening. When I went over to Clinton's house there were two men in the living room. One was middle-aged with grey hair and glasses, quite tall. He stood up and introduced himself as a senior member of the INLA. The other man was in his late twenties to mid-thirties, fairly stout, black hair with a side parting. He was unshaven and had a scar on the side of his face. He had heavy, inset eyes. He was wearing jeans, baseball boots, a sweatshirt and a ski jacket. I did not know this man's name at the time, but he introduced himself as a senior INLA man.

'They began to ask me a lot of questions as to how I had come to be at a party and about various people around. It became apparent that they suspected me of being some kind of informer. Mary Clinton brought in coffee and food but I ate nothing. I noticed that she locked the door behind her. There was no other way out of the room. I was questioned until quite late and was then moved to a nearby house by "the fat man" and another man who had arrived – a man with a mask who was tall, with a big nose – and the grey-haired man. I was detained in this other house for about two days during which I was interrogated on and off by various people, including "the fat man". At times I was blindfolded and sometimes not. At no time did I admit giving police any assistance, and insisted that I did not know anything anyway.

'After two days I was blindfolded again, stripped and moved once more. I think this occurred about 11pm. By this time I had got to know their voices and recognised the voice of "the fat man". I could also see through the blindfold which was not very effective, made of a wide knot cotton material. Eventually "the fat man" untied me and took off the blindfold and informed me to get dressed as I was going to be moved again. He tied me up again when I had been dressed and left the room for a short while during which I had untied myself. He came in and saw this and blindfolded me. He led me out of the house, banging my head against a wall on the way causing my nose to bleed. This was done with considerable force. I was pushed under something into a room and told to stand in the corner. I turned round and saw him move back and heard a clicking noise. Very shortly afterwards I heard three shots and fell to the ground. I looked up again and saw "the fat man", who stood for a short while before moving away. I lay bleeding for a while before crawling out of the house and running towards the maternity hospital.

'When interviewed by police following this incident I gave a full description of the man who I called "the fat man", the man who shot me. I also drew a photofit of the man for the police while in hospital. I gave this to [three policemen]. When I gave them the photofit they all appeared to know the man and laughed, saying that it was a very good likeness. I asked them if they knew the man but they said that they didn't, which I thought was odd.

'I was kept under police protection, which I did not ask for. I was told that I would have to give evidence. When I let them know that I did not want to give evidence they indicated that they would make my life very difficult, that they could charge me with a number of offences like collecting information for terrorists, because I had associated with them. They were particularly interested in William Mulhall, whom they said was an IRA man. They also said that they would spread it around paramilitary circles that I was an informer and there would be a race to see who would get me first.

'I felt intimidated by all this and felt like a prisoner. They had my driving licence, passport and all my papers. They refused to give me my passport back. They told me that they would "reallocate" me, give me £10,000 plus the £2,860 the INLA took from my property. I was kept for a while in Lisburn Army barracks and also in a block of flats in England where there were other people and their families in similar situations. I was kept there until after the trial. I was given £30 drinking money and groceries bought for me. Policemen also lived in the complex who kept a constant watch on you and who wouldn't let you out of the building without their permission. I was given all sorts of promises and began getting very frustrated and angry.

'Eventually they gave me a passport in a new name and put me on a plane to France. It took some time before I got any money from them. I had set myself up in France with the proceeds of my NIO claim, £36,000. My family solicitor, Mr R Barbour of White, McMillan and Wheeler, acted for me in this. I was in an impossible position – I was never an informer and never asked or wanted to be kept in police custody. I believed I had no choice in the matter. The police know my address in France – I am constantly getting in touch with them to give me a proper ID. All I have is a passport, a name and a driving licence which I forced them to give me when I was charged with driving offences in England. (I do spend a lot of time in England as I have now married and my wife stays here.)

'After the arrest of Morrison and others I was made aware that the man they were accused of holding was the man who shot me. I did not know his name however. I was told this on the quiet by one of the police minders with whom I had become particularly friendly. I do not wish to name him, as our friendship greatly annoyed his superiors.

'Some time later, roughly a year ago, I was approached by police and asked to make myself available at Earl's Court police station. I thought this was to finally settle my dispute about relocation money. I kept the appointment and was met by three policemen. It turned out that they wanted to talk about my shooting. They were particularly interested in my description of the man who shot me. They indicated that they might have had somebody. I told them all about giving a detailed description to police at the time and about the photofit I gave to [the police] at the time. I knew by this time the circumstances and suggested to them that they were protecting a man working for them, and that they knew exactly who he was. They went very pale and cold towards me. They sent me out of the room. When they brought me back they asked if I would attend an ID parade and would I look at photos. I agreed if they sorted out my other grievances. Not long after that an officer came over and gave me £4,000. I still have never been given a full ID – like a history, birth certificate and so on. I did bring the matter up of identifying the man who shot me but he would make no comment. I never heard any more about it.

'On the day of Morrison's conviction I was watching TV news in England and saw the photos of "Sandy" Lynch. I immediately recognised him as the man who shot me. I phoned C14 [the relocation unit of the RUC] and left a message on the machine that he was the man who shot me. I also got [a policeman] at Ballymena RUC station and told him. He panicked and said he would look into it. In the next few days I contacted Mr Barbour, my solicitor in Belfast, who advised me to go to a police station in England and report the matter, which I did. I asked for a superintendent and told him who I was and what I wanted to say. He went off to check, but when he came back told me that he was told by RUC not to take a statement and that they were looking into it. Before this I had contacted several journalists ... I would like to see Lynch prosecuted and to get compensation from Lynch personally.'

Morrison's lawyers had, it seemed, obtained a statement which, if true, would blow the entire prosecution case wide open. The judge at the original trial, Lord Chief Justice Sir Brian Hutton, had accepted that Lynch was a worthless liar who would say anything to cover his own tracks. Now here was someone who would testify that he was the victim of an attempted murder carried out by a man working for Special Branch, and therefore in clear breach of both the law and agent-handling guidelines. This witness would also say that police were aware of that attempted murder.

More crucial for the Morrison case was Duggan's claim that he attempted over and over again to expose 'the fat man' and that even as Morrison and his co-accused were in jail awaiting trial, Duggan was making his claims to serving RUC officers. There is no suggestion whatsoever that the CID officers involved in the Morrison case were aware of the trips to London by colleagues trying to deal with Duggan's grievances.

The mystery of Peter Duggan remains. Friends believe he is still living in France. Others place him in London. Wherever he is, he disappeared shortly after giving his startling statement to Morrison's lawyers and he failed to appear at the Court of Appeal hearing in 1992. One security force insider believes he was paid off by someone in Special Branch to keep quiet so that he wouldn't appear for Morrison at the Appeal. If this was the case, and there is no evidence either way, it was a clear perversion of the course of justice. Only Peter Duggan knows the answers. Only he can solve the mystery. It's time he came forward and explained.

✳ ✳ ✳

There is another disturbing aspect to the entire Morrison case which only emerged in November 2003. In August 2002 Ingram met with two investigators from the Office of the Police Ombudsman. The Ombudsman's representatives were led by Martin Bridger, an officer with a fine track record for investigating allegations of malpractice. During that meeting Ingram alleged that Morrison had been the victim of entrapment – that an agent other than Lynch was involved in setting up Morrison, aided and abetted by the FRU and by

RUC Special Branch, who ran the operation. We now know of course that the agent was Freddie Scappaticci. Ingram, while no fan of Morrison, believed there had been malpractice by Special Branch – allowing Lynch to remain captive in a house for up to twenty-four hours after Scappaticci had left the premises was cruel and unjustifiable; Scappaticci's handler, a good friend of Martin Ingram's, had said so in numerous heated telephone conversations with Special Branch that weekend. Scappaticci's handler accused Special Branch of using Lynch as human bait.

Ingram had another concern for them. He suspected that Special Branch had withheld information on the case from its CID officers, who began investigating Lynch's detention straight after the raid on the house. Ingram suspected too that the defence, the prosecution and the trial judge had not been informed that Scappaticci was in fact a State agent and was thus involved in the entrapment of Morrison. The Ombudsman's officers began their investigation after receiving a complaint from Ingram.

In January 2003, a further meeting took place between Ingram and two Ombudsman investigators, one of the original officers and a new officer. Ingram was assured that their investigations to that date had established that the trial judge had not been given all of the information on the case. Ingram expressed his concerns, not that Morrison was an innocent party, but that the rule of law had been breached and it was important that their inquiries were swiftly concluded. The officers seemed to be in full agreement, but said that ultimately it would be down to the Ombudsman, Nuala O'Loan. Despite assurances that they would keep Ingram up to date with the inquiry, no further information was forthcoming. In a phone call in March 2003, Ingram was told that the Ombudsman was not going to proceed with the case – it had instead been handed over to the Stevens Inquiry. Ingram has never been approached by Sir John subsequent to that day.

It would be more than six months before we learned exactly what had happened with the Ombudsman's investigation. The Ombudsman herself had only ever issued a short statement, in which she said that her officers had found no evidence of malpractice by police officers. Her office did in fact discover that while CID submitted its file to the Director of Public Prosecutions, RUC Special Branch submitted separate documentation. That documentation stated that Scappaticci was a security force agent, and included a request for this information to be withheld from the prosecution, the defence and the Lord Chief Justice, as a matter of national security.

The DPP's office agreed to that request and issued a Public Interest Certificate. To withhold evidence from a criminal trial, knowing that this evidence will alter the entire thrust of the defence case, would seem to most reasonable people to be a miscarriage of justice. This is what the Ombudsman found, but her investigators could not pursue it any further as her remit covers investigations into the police only.

Bridger took a different view. Reliable sources say Bridger was very uncomfortable with the actions of Special Branch and believed that what they did bordered on malpractice, but he left the Ombudsman's office to take up a new role with the Metropolitan police before completing his inquiries. Shortly afterwards, Sir John Stevens took over the case with the agreement of O'Loan. She hadn't found evidence of malpractice, as her inquiry hadn't been completed. Sir John, who has known the identity of Stakeknife for at least four years, now has primacy in the Morrison/Lynch investigation.

Chapter 8

The Real Brian Nelson

Harkin

If Freddie Scappaticci was the biggest catch for the FRU from the republican side, then Brian Nelson was one of its best assets within the loyalist paramilitaries. Over the years, Brian Nelson has been variously portrayed as a heroic life-saver, a misguided double agent who found himself trapped in circumstances beyond his control, and a sectarian mur-derer. Today his name has become synonymous with sectari-anism and murder.

But to understand the real Brian Nelson one must look at where he came from and his activities before his 'sudden' emergence in the Ulster Defence Association (UDA) in the mid-1980s. One must also understand how he functioned within the British system of anti-terror operations. The infor-mation in this chapter on the early life of Brian Nelson is based on interviews over fourteen years with friends and fellow UDA members of Nelson who knew him intimately. Before I broke the story of Brian Nelson in the *Sunday News* in 1990 I pursued many individuals who knew him. Among them was the UDA brigadier Tommy Lyttle, who has since died. As the scope of Nelson's activities became clearer in 1992, many loyalist individuals were happy to talk about someone they saw as a 'tout'. More than a decade after

Nelson's conviction, I re-interviewed those who were still willing to talk. A former soldier who followed Nelson from the British Army into the paramilitaries also helped provide details that others would not.

My investigations have taken me to ex-soldiers who served with Nelson in the Black Watch regiment and, more importantly, to the loyalists who worked alongside him in the years before his recruitment by military intelligence. It is a story which the British State would rather wasn't told to the world. It is an insight into how low the British government had sunk in its quest to defeat paramilitarism and sectarianism.

Nelson was born in the hard-line loyalist Shankill district of west Belfast in 1947. One of six children, he was never academically gifted, and was described in school reports as 'lazy'. His lack of ambition was perhaps partly due to his father's position at the Harland & Wolff shipyard, where widespread discrimination and 'fixing' meant that sons of workers were almost guaranteed apprenticeships. As a Protestant, Brian Nelson also had more right to a job than any Catholic applicant. When he left school at the age of fifteen, Nelson, like many of his friends, walked straight into a job at the shipyard. And, like many Protestant teenagers of the day, he took the privilege of such job-fixing for granted, lasting just sixteen months into a four-year joinery apprenticeship. Colleagues at the time remember him as a loner who found it hard to mix with others, a young man who, just as in school, was extremely lazy. 'Brian would run a mile rather than do any work,' said 'Jim', a former co-worker who spoke to me. 'He'd spend as much time doing errands as possible and was always heading off for a smoke. To this day I honestly don't believe Brian could hang a door. He wasn't interested at all.'

His decision to quit the post his father had secured for him led to a rift that never healed. 'We knew we (Protestants) were privileged, in that there was always a job at the ship-yard, but even so it was frowned upon that anyone, never mind somebody so young, would throw away an apprenticeship like that. But some did and Brian was one of them. I think when you take something for granted you don't appreciate it and Brian never appreciated it. I don't think Brian's father ever forgave him, and I don't think Brian gave a damn,' said the former Harland & Wolff worker.

It was early 1964 and, like everywhere else in these islands, Belfast was swinging to the music of the Sixties. Catholics and Protestants socialised together in the city-centre pubs and ballrooms, dancing to the music of the showbands. But in Northern Ireland there was something different about it all – the politics of the day were never far away; you only had to scratch the surface to touch the bitterness and hatred, the division and the sectarianism. The Northern Ireland Civil Rights Association was demanding equal voting rights for all – 'one man, one vote'– in a country where landowners and business people, mainly Protestants, had multiple votes.

For a man with a reputation for being lazy and having an acute inability to stick to any task, Brian Nelson chose a rather peculiar path – he joined the British Army. More peculiar still was the regiment he picked – the Royal Highland Regiment, more commonly known as the Black Watch. It is one of the British Army's toughest regiments, with a proud history dating from 1725. Thousands of soldiers from the Black Watch were lost in both world wars and it was the last British regiment to serve in Hong Kong before the colony was handed back to China in 1997. The Black Watch recruits heavily in Perthshire, Fife, Dundee and Angus in Scotland, but it wasn't unusual for it to accept recruits from elsewhere in Britain and Northern Ireland.

Brian Nelson's four-and-a-half years in the Black Watch were chequered, to say the least. 'Sammy', a one-time friend who spoke with Nelson in a Belfast bar just before he joined the British Army, told me: 'I knew a bit about the Army, because my father had served during the war. I asked my dad how he thought Brian would get on and he laughed and said, "He won't survive a week with the Black Watch." When I told Brian he just shrugged, saying there was nothing better to do.'

But, by hook or by crook, Brian Nelson managed to survive one of the toughest regiments of the British Army for four years. I have spoken to soldiers who served with him and, according to them, Nelson was just about the most disobedient, rebellious recruit in the barracks. He was constantly going AWOL (absent without leave). When he did have authorised leave, he would return late. He often fell asleep on duty. 'Brian was always getting caught for something,' says one former colleague. 'I think he was picked on by some officers because he wasn't Scottish, but then they didn't need an excuse. It was a miracle Brian Nelson survived for so long. On one occasion in Perth he was picked up by the police after starting a fight in one of the town's bars. He was punished with all the usual tasks, but it never seemed to bother him. He was a great deal tougher than many people thought, for he took a lot of crap over the years.'

According to this former colleague, Nelson 'was always passing comment on the news from Northern Ireland. I do remember one occasion, which stuck with me, him referring to Catholics as "Taigs". He muttered something along the lines of, "Those Taigs need to be sorted out." With our own sectarianism in Scotland, I knew what he was talking about.'

In early 1969 Nelson left the Black Watch, under circumstances that are not fully clear. It was a relief both to himself and the British Army. He was twenty-two years old and, despite an upbringing by parents who had close Catholic friends – his mother was involved in the Peace People, an organisation co-founded by Mairead Corrigan, Betty Williams and Ciaran McKeown following a horrific incident in August 1976, when the three children of Corrigan's sister were killed – he was soon involved in paramilitary activities. He became an avid follower of Ian Paisley and, as violence spread across Northern Ireland and vigilante groups sprang up, Nelson set up and ran his own 'battalion' of Paisley's Ulster Protestant Volunteer Force (UPVF), which, as Paisley had demanded, vowed to save Ulster 'from Rome'.

Nelson gained respect in north and west Belfast for the way he drilled new recruits into this paramilitary force, established, it was claimed, to 'protect' Protestant areas from attack. Brian Nelson could not have been happier. He was earning the respect of gullible teenage recruits, a respect he never received in the Black Watch, and a respect he would, incredibly, gain again from the British Army fifteen years later. Within eighteen months, like most of those who joined the UPVF, he was working for the Ulster Defence Association (UDA), Northern Ireland's largest paramilitary group, set up to draw together the loyalist vigilante groups which were dotted around Northern Ireland.

Those who knew Nelson at the time remember a 'dedicated' member of the terror group. Not surprisingly, they were reluctant to detail the level of his involvement in the UDA, although one former member confirmed that Nelson had been involved in murders. This former UDA man, who has long since severed his links with the loyalist group, said he would not implicate others in what happened at that time. 'But those days were mad and the Troubles were young and no one really knew where we were all headed. But yes, Brian Nelson was involved in the taking of lives. The exact number I cannot go into. But yes, he was involved, like many, many others. The fact he was an ex-soldier meant that he was called upon more than most. He had a deal of respect because he could handle firearms better than most, and he was always keen to impress the bosses.'

Nelson's status as an 'ex-soldier' has been the subject of conflicting claims. Another former UDA member claimed that Nelson had not been booted out of the British Army as has been officially recorded. 'Nelson told me once never to repeat it, but that he had gone AWOL from the Black Watch in sixty-nine and was a wanted man,' said this former associate. This is a scenario suspected by the Stevens Inquiry team, who later investigated the affair, as well as by many loyalists who were prominent at the time. The Black Watch refused to cooperate with this book, so it is impossible to verify Nelson's status at that time, but in the years 1972 and 1973 the people of Northern Ireland saw the very worst days of the Troubles, from Bloody Sunday in Derry to Bloody Friday in Belfast. Hundreds died and Brian Nelson was in the thick of it.

'Brian was up for anything that was going,' said a former comrade. 'He was a small, almost weedy man. It clearly helped his ego when he was given a job to do, and he was given many jobs to do.'

Brian Nelson was not, as has been said in British government-approved accounts, a misguided individual on the fringes of a paramilitary gang. In March 1973, Nelson's role inside the UDA would finally be exposed for what it was.

✳ ✳ ✳

The war in Northern Ireland had by now claimed more than 800 lives. The weekend beginning Friday, 23 March 1973 marked another horrific increase in the slaughter. Two women, both members of the IRA, lured four soldiers to a flat on Belfast's Antrim Road. The flat had been rented some time before by the Provisionals. The women had met up with the soldiers at a hotel in Lisburn and invited them to a 'house--warming party' at the flat. The women, who used the names Jean and Pat, were waiting with a third woman when the soldiers – all Catholics – arrived. Drinks and sandwiches were served. A fire burned brightly in the grate and candles glowed across the living room. The soldiers were glad of the hospitality, and were not in the least bit suspicious when one of the women left the party, claiming to be going to get a fourth girl to make up the numbers.

When the door opened again, twenty minutes later, she was accompanied by two armed and masked IRA men. All four soldiers were bound, gagged and dragged to a bedroom where they were forced to lie face-down on a bed. The Provisionals cocked their weapons and opened fire with a machine gun and a pistol. Staff Sergeant Barrington Joseph Foster, twenty-eight, of the Duke of Edinburgh's Royal Regiment, and Sergeant Michael Muldoon, a twenty-five-year-old dental technician, died at the scene. Thomas Penrose, twenty-eight, a sergeant with the Royal Corps of Signals, died several hours later in hospital. A fourth soldier injured in the shooting survived. It was the second time in two years that three soldiers had been murdered in a so-called 'honey-trap'.

In a statement, the Citizens Defence Committee, an anti-violence civil rights organisation, said: 'What cause can retain a vestige of morality when its pursuit results in Irishmen and women reducing themselves as human beings to the point where they participate in this horror.' It was a truly shocking incident, but it was just one of many that weekend. Bomb attacks in those days made single sentences in the morning papers. The death of a police officer wounded in an incident the month before was barely a headline.

On that weekend alone, three other soldiers were injured in a landmine explosion near Crossmaglen, a soldier was injured in a shooting in north Belfast and across the city on the Falls Road a gunman was shot. In Rosslea in County Fermanagh, gunmen opened fire with rockets and machine guns on a British Army base, while another rocket narrowly missed an Army jeep in Newtownhamilton. In Strabane, County Tyrone, two civilians were slightly injured when a bomb exploded in a shop, while in Newry a Protestant farm was set ablaze in a sectarian attack. Derry saw dozens of incidents, including shootings and bombings, and in Larne soldiers arrested three youths who had tried to burn down St MacNissi's Catholic church. In Lisburn, windows in the home of former unionist MP Richard Ferguson QC were blown out after a bomb attack on a nearby pipe factory

On that Sunday night, 25 March 1973, there was another incident which didn't even make it into the next edition of the *Belfast Telegraph*, such was the mayhem of the times. Gerry Higgins, a forty-two-year-old, partially-sighted Catholic from Duncairn Parade in the New Lodge district of north Belfast, was busy as usual, trying to prevent the sort of trouble which had engulfed everyday life in Belfast. As a peace campaigner he had been instrumental in a unique scheme still being copied at interface areas to this day; he had set up a network with Protestants in Duncairn Gardens aimed at easing tensions and bringing together residents from both sides for peace talks. Higgins, according to those in the New Lodge who remember him, was a mild-mannered man who despaired at the times he found himself in.

At 10pm on 25 March, Gerry Higgins was walking home alone along North Queen Street after a night out, heading in a direction that clearly marked him out as a Catholic. That evening, Brian Nelson, now twenty-five years old and working as a driver, and John Eppleston, seventeen, unemployed and from Malvern Street in Shankill, were among a crowd of around sixty UDA members and supporters drinking at the UDA club in Wilton Street. Most people there had been discussing the weekend's events and talking about taking 'revenge' for the murder of the soldiers in the Antrim Road flat. Brian Nelson took action. He approached his UDA commander with a plan to 'get a Taig', knowing it would be greeted with immediate approval.

Within minutes, he and Eppleston were driving towards the nationalist New Lodge area, less than a mile away, hunting for a victim. This area had already seen the abductions of many Catholics, and many more would follow. Driving along North Queen Street, they soon came across Gerry Higgins and pulled up alongside him. Higgins didn't have time to run. Nelson and Eppleston jumped out, put a gun to their victim's head and forced him to lie on the back seat of their Hillman Minx car with a coat over his head. He was driven back to the Wilton Street club and frog-marched past punters to a room at the rear where he was to suffer horrific torture.

Nelson and Eppleston held an arm each as Higgins was tied to a chair. The victim's shoes were removed and over the period of the next hour he was beaten repeatedly all over his body. As the blows rained down, up to six UDA men questioned him over and over again about the IRA, about who he knew in the New Lodge and about who his friends were. Higgins had no connections with paramilitary groups, other than those he spoke to on both sides when trying to diffuse tensions. He couldn't answer their questions, so Nelson decided to take the torture to another level.

Nelson was a prolific smoker and he chain-smoked throughout the interrogation, moving the lighted cigarette from his mouth to the head of Gerry Higgins. Next, a hand-operated generator was brought in. Higgins was tied across a beer barrel and forced to hold the two electric terminals. When the pain became too much for Higgins and he lost his grip, Nelson and his cohorts wet their victim's hands and tied the terminals to them. The shocks – sometimes up to 100 volts – continued for some time. Every now and then some of the forty or so UDA members in the club would come in and take turns at hitting Higgins. His assailants included women.

Police sources say that it was Nelson who suggested that Higgins should be killed. Officers who briefed counsel for his subsequent trial said there was no doubt that the loyalist was the ringleader. Nelson now won approval from his UDA commander for Higgins to die. The Catholic was taken back out onto Wilton Street, where he was told by Nelson that he was being released – this tactic was often used by paramilitary jailers in order to relax a prisoner about to die, and so avoid a struggle. John Eppleston and Samuel James Brown, then eighteen and from Pernau Street, grabbed their victim as Nelson removed a diary from Higgins's pocket. Nelson opened the first page of the diary and wrote: 'This is the first to go. Two to follow.'

There is absolutely no question what Brian Nelson had in mind. They had a gun. They had a Catholic and that Catholic was going to die. But Gerry Higgins was not going quietly. He had just been through hell in that UDA torture chamber, and he began to struggle as Nelson, Brown and Eppleston bundled him into the back of the car. The tussle alerted soldiers on foot patrol a few hundred yards away, and two Land Rovers sped in and blocked the car. Nelson and his two UDA cohorts were arrested. Higgins, in a clearly distressed state, was rushed to the Royal Victoria Hospital for treatment. He was very seriously ill for many weeks, and his wife Claire says he never recovered from the attack.

Mrs Higgins, who still lives in north Belfast, told me: 'Gerry died in 1980, eight years after what happened. I don't think he was ever right after that, but he never wanted to discuss what happened. I'd say that was because he didn't want to upset me or himself.' His son, Gary, spoke for the first time about the incident following the death of Brian Nelson in April 2003. 'My dad was registered as blind and they even took his heart tablets. He was tortured and beaten to a pulp by both men and women. Finally, they took him outside to shoot him where he put up a struggle. A patrol from 42 Marine Commandos were coming along the street and they thought it was a pub brawl. They put everybody up against the wall and my dad told a soldier that the guy at the end had a gun. So the gang, including Nelson, were arrested. My dad was critically ill for weeks after. When he finally got out, he was never the same man. He died in 1980 and he was just forty-nine. You'll not see his name in *Lost Lives* as a victim of the Troubles, but I know Nelson and that gang killed him.'

Gary said he had 'no nasty feelings' for Nelson now that he is dead, and added: 'There's no point dancing on his grave. He's got to meet his maker and answer for his crimes.'

In later years, Nelson's Army handlers would express surprise that so many innocent non-combatants died as a result of his intelligence work. It is my contention that Brian Nelson was always a sectarian bigot who enjoyed the targeting and killing of Catholics; that the Brian Nelson who beat, burned and electrocuted Gerry Higgins in 1973 was psychologically the same man who sent paramilitary gunmen out to take the lives of up to eighty people a decade-and-a-half later.

Nelson, Brown and Eppleston were all initially charged with conspiracy to murder, along with a host of other offences. In his statement to police, Nelson claimed that although they were not going to release Higgins as they had promised him, they were, in fact, going to hand him over to unnamed persons. Police did not believe him. A deal was done. The conspiracy charges were dropped in return for guilty pleas to lesser charges of intimidation, possession with intent and actual bodily harm. Nelson was sentenced to seven years.

Eppleston, who admitted the same charges, got just two years. Brown didn't even go to jail. He was given a one-year suspended sentence, for possession of a weapon with intent and intimidation. At the sentencing hearing at Belfast City Commission on Monday, 18 February 1974, the court was given varying accounts of what had happened eleven months earlier. Crown counsel Robert Babington QC accepted that there was not enough evidence to prove the loyalist trio had planned to kill Higgins. It was, however, a 'manifestly political and sectarian' incident, he told the court, and Mr Higgins had been told he was going to be shot.

Defending the trio, Robert McCartney QC said it was a rather 'ghastly' offence, but that Nelson had used his own car and had made no effort to disguise it. Eppleston, he said, was only told of the abduction plan in North Queen Street. This is disputed by loyalist sources, but their lawyer had to take their claims at face value. There was no evidence to the contrary.

McCartney described the kidnapping as 'bungling' and 'amateurish'. Nelson showed no remorse for his part in the plot. Eppleston shouted 'No Surrender' to the assembled supporters at the City Commission hearing. Both went straight into the UDA compound at Long Kesh to serve their sentences.

'There is no doubt in my mind that Brian was going to kill that man that night,' said a UDA member who shared the compound. 'Everybody swapped stories inside about what happened to them and why they were there, and Brian was no different. He told me he was ordered to kill Higgins and plans were made to abduct two more Catholics in the following days as a response to the soldiers' murders. When he was questioned of course he denied this, but that is what you do and they [the RUC] couldn't prove otherwise.'

Nelson was back on the streets and back in the UDA by Christmas 1977. In sanitised accounts of his life, it appears that Brian Nelson did nothing in the years between his release and his decision to leave Northern Ireland in 1981. But nothing could be further from the truth. It was at this time, according to well-placed loyalist sources, that he began collating information on targets for UDA murder gangs. He took a job as a carpet fitter and travelled freely between nationalist and loyalist areas, carrying out surveillance work as he went. It was work which would take on more significance when Nelson, agent number 6137, was given a job that was paid for by British taxpayers – setting up Catholics for murder.

Chapter 9

A Litany of Death: Agent 6137

Ingram/Harkin

Gerry Adams, MP for west Belfast and Sinn Féin president, walked briskly from the Magistrates' Court in central Belfast, slowed only for a few seconds by photographers and camera crews. Four minders escorted him towards his car, which was waiting just outside the pedestrian security zone. They were all on high alert – they knew they were in a vulnerable area, given the level of publicity surrounding the RUC's ongoing court case against Adams on obstruction charges. They knew there was a distinct possibility that loyalists might try to launch an assassination bid. Once inside the gold-coloured Ford Cortina car, they sped off in the direction of west Belfast, towards City Hall.

Adams and his minders weren't the only people feeling nervous that Wednesday lunchtime on 14 March 1984. The British Army and MI5 were about to take an enormous risk by allowing UFF gunmen to launch a murder bid on the high-profile MP.

As Adams's car travelled along Howard Street, less than half a mile from the courthouse, three UFF gunmen struck. They pulled up alongside the Cortina in their stolen Rover car and riddled it with bullets. Adams, sitting in the middle of the back seat, was hit in the neck, back and arm. Most seriously injured was Sean Keenan, who was hit in the face and lost several teeth. Also hurt were Joe Keenan and Kevin Rooney. The fifth occupant and driver of the car, Bob Murray, was unhurt. Undercover members of the security forces watched the entire incident. They allowed the attack to take place, but when the shooting ceased they swooped on the three loyalist gunmen within seconds. Gerald Welsh, John Gregg and Colin Gray, all from Rathcoole, a large loyalist housing estate in north Belfast, were apprehended in nearby Wellington Place as they fled the scene in the Rover. Gregg was wounded, having been shot, by mistake, by Welsh.

Several eyewitnesses described the events. One said: 'When I arrived [at the scene] there were two cars, one Ford and one Rover, sitting with the doors open. A uniformed policeman was holding a man very firmly against the railings, with other RUC men standing over what appeared to be two suspects spreadeagled on the footpath. I was later told that one of the men taken from the car had been shot accidentally. It all happened very quickly. The streets were packed with shoppers and many people were badly shocked.'

Adams and his colleagues were driven to the Royal Victoria Hospital for treatment. In a Press statement released by RUC headquarters, the security forces described the arrest operation as 'fortuitous' – officers had been in the right place at the right time. Journalists were briefed about 'heroic' members of the security forces who had helped to catch the Adams plotters. Some were explained as off-duty members of the security forces who had simply happened upon the scene. On Thursday, 15 March 1984 the *Belfast Telegraph* reported:

'The Secretary of State Mr [James] Prior has no plans to make any special statement on the shooting of the Sinn Féin MP and the Northern Ireland Office's attitude is that it should be left to the security forces [to comment on]. Concern that the IRA has been engaged in a new campaign to create sectarian strife in the province emerged in an RUC headquarters' statement early this week, and Ministers share the concern of reprisals between loyalist and republican paramilitaries [following the attempted murder of Adams]. Mr Prior said on Tuesday [13 March, the day before the attack] that covert operations had recently been stepped up – not in Border areas but in various parts of Northern Ireland. Officials are adamant that the speedy arrests following yesterday's shooting were coincidental.'

But Adams, speaking to reporters from his hospital bed, concluded that there must have been collusion between the gunmen and the security forces: 'I don't think it was a British Army operation, but I do think they were aware of it. It is otherwise inconceivable that there were so many plain-clothes security men about.' He wasn't to know until many years later the full extent of that collusion.

The day after the incident, Bob Murray told reporters that Adams's party had requested access to the court buildings from the rear, in order to remove him from the area as quickly as possible: 'We did this because we knew there was a security problem. We were told by court officials that such an arrangement could not be made. We had, however, taken our own precautions by staggering our arrival time and our leaving time when we had to go to court. Yesterday the court was late in rising for lunch and I thought because of this that it was fair enough to assume that we were all right – you wouldn't expect people to wait in a car with guns beyond the normal time. I think the gunmen must have been waiting opposite the courthouse for us to leave and then followed us.' He was right: they had been.

News of the shooting and Adams's survival was greeted with delight at RUC headquarters in Belfast and at FRU headquarters in Lisburn, but one man did not share that feeling: Brian Nelson, UDA intelligence officer and FRU spy. Nelson had been involved in the plot to kill Gerry Adams and, make no mistake about it, he wanted Adams dead. He had warned his handlers in advance that the attempt would take place, but he fully expected Adams to die in the shooting. Unknown to Nelson, his handlers had decided that Adams should live, or at least that they would take measures to give the Sinn Féin leader a chance of surviving. Thanks to information supplied by Nelson and another agent, the FRU knew that the UFF hit team would include John Gregg (the UDA's top hitman in the area, who was subsequently murdered in a loyalist feud in 2003), and it knew where the weapons were being kept. The security forces were able to get their hands on the bullets and the weapons the UFF were going to use on the day, which were being stored in a shed in Rathcoole. FRU officers 'jarked' the weapons – which involved reducing the charge in the bullets and thereby reducing their impact when fired – and replaced them as they had found them, so the would-be assassins had no idea they had been tampered with. The gunmen managed to fire twelve rounds at Adams's car before the guns jammed. After the shooting, Nelson contacted his handlers and in a subsequent meeting berated them for saving Adams's life. Nelson knew the charges in the bullets had been reduced and that it was this that had saved Adams's and Keenan's lives. He had, albeit unwittingly, helped to save the leader of the republican movement. During a heated argument, Nelson swore that the next time the UFF targeted Adams, he wouldn't warn his handlers.

There has been some speculation in the Press as to why the FRU saved Gerry Adams's life in 1984, or at least gambled that he would be spared. There are two popular explanations. One is that the British knew that Adams wanted to take the republican movement into politics and away from violence and preserved his life to further that aim. The other is that the FRU couldn't have prevented the UFF attack at an earlier stage as it would have risked exposing Nelson to the UDA/UFF, and in 1984 the FRU very much needed Brian Nelson in place because he was their only agent inside loyalism. Allowing the murder bid to go ahead would stave off any suspicions. They gambled that their immediate explanation of security force activity just prior to the assassination attempt would help to provide some cover. The FRU's reasoning in deciding to throw Adams a lifeline can be summed up quite simply as a case of 'better the devil you know...'

Nelson's handlers had yet again 'played God' with someone's life. It was a calculated risk, a gamble with very high stakes and it was largely luck that brought about a good result for the security forces: Adams wounded but saved; Nelson still an asset; Adams's would-be killers behind bars.

Brian Nelson's role in the attempt on Adams's life has been noted before, but his overall role within the FRU and the UDA at that time has yet to be fully described. From conversations with senior FRU officers, Ingram learned that Brian Nelson was recruited not in 1987, as has been widely reported, but in 1979, after his release from prison (that is, if he wasn't already an agent in 1974 when he set out to kill Gerry Higgins). This has been confirmed by loyalist sources from the time. His exact role in these years, ie, 1978–1982, is still a matter of speculation due to insufficient files available, but we do know that in 1981 and 1982 Nelson was an agent for 2 Company in Germany, where he spied on the Irish community for both the British Army and MI6. However, the Army was anxious to get him back to Northern Ireland. In late 1982, Ingram had a conversation with a senior FRU officer about Nelson and the message was clear: the FRU wanted to bring Nelson 'back from Germany to infiltrate the UDA/UFF', the implication being that he had previously worked for the FRU in Northern Ireland. That conversation also touched on another pressing issue: the RUC's insistence that it should be the only branch of the security forces to recruit loyalists. By Christmas 1982, however, the FRU had won the argument – Nelson was a serving British soldier and, as such, an employee of the Ministry of Defence, therefore the FRU was entitled to use him.

Brian Nelson returned to Northern Ireland and quickly re-established himself inside the UDA, taking on a valuable role gathering intelligence for UDA/UFF units throughout the greater Belfast area. By mid-1983 he was the man responsible for naming and framing most of those who were targeted and killed by the UDA from then until October 25 1985, when he left Northern Ireland for another stint in Germany. We should point out that during this two-year period, Nelson's information was used by the FRU in a different way from the manner in which it was handled during the period from 1987 to 1990. Between 1983 and 1985 many UDA/UFF terror operations were stopped or compromised by various means. The facts speak for themselves: during the last six months of 1983 the UDA in Belfast did not kill any nationalists or Catholics. It is our understanding that at that time Nelson's information was used to prevent a number of murder attempts (a very different *modus operandi* from that implemented by the regime he was to work for in the late 1980s). It wasn't that Nelson wasn't itching to kill, but rather that his handlers at the time used his information to save lives rather than to take them.

It was inevitable, however, that 'sacrifices' would be made and that Nelson's role would lead to deaths. On the morning of 16 November 1984, Nelson's intelligence report for the UDA on Catholic milkman Patrick Brady was used by loyalist hitman Michael Stone. Brady was to be Stone's first murder victim, and the first killing initiated by Nelson in what would be a long and bloody career in the UDA. In a later statement to the police, Stone confirmed reading a military intelligence report on Brady, who was a member of Sinn Féin. In the statement, which was read at Stone's trial for the murder several years later, Stone described the murder:

> 'The target for us that morning was a big fellow called Brady who was a milkroundsman whom I had seen on video attending the [Sinn Féin] *ard fheis* in Dublin. I remember him standing with his arms folded across his chest. I had read an intelligence sheet on him which stated that he was using his milk round to gain knowledge of where the police and Army were living and he

would then pass on this information to the Provos. I was told that he drove a white car and was due to arrive at the dairy at half six or a quarter to seven. The driver said to us after about twenty minutes, "There he is." Our driver then [drove] up beside him and stopped about three feet from him. I shot him twice in the body as we started to drive off. He fell on the road. I fired a third shot at him. The others said to shoot the helper, but he was too young and I didn't do it. This was my first job. That's how I can remember the details.'

Patrick Brady was thirty-six, married, with two children. Republican sources insist he worked for Sinn Féin and had no involvement with the Provisional IRA. This claim is contrary to the information contained in the military intelligence report on Brady. It's not clear how this report came about, but it seems, according to senior loyalist sources, that Nelson generated the report but did not inform his handlers that he had passed it on to the UDA and, via the UDA, to Stone.

Brady was the only victim of Brian Nelson's intelligence-gathering activities between 1983 and 1985. It is claimed by FRU officers that Nelson was kept under close scrutiny throughout these years and that his information was used to save dozens of lives. The same could not be said of Nelson's next period as an FRU informant, when he returned to Northern Ireland from Regensburg, Bavaria, just before Christmas 1986. Over the following three years he would not only be allowed to kill but actively encouraged to kill. The game had changed. Nelson was now used for what one senior FRU officer called 'proper targeting', and his victims were largely innocent Catholics.

＊＊＊

Brian Nelson's murder victims have been the subject of a number of probes, most notably by the BBC investigative journalist John Ware, whose tireless research into Nelson's activities has generated a number of chilling documentaries. But the full list of those who died as a result of Nelson's role can only now be published for the first time. In his 2003 report, Sir John Stevens concluded that Brian Nelson played an active role in, and that there was conspiracy between Nelson and the UDA/UFF in, the murders of fifteen people between 1986 and 1989. He also had a role in fourteen attempted murders and sixty-two other murder conspiracies, including direct involvement in the attempted murder of Alex Maskey, who would later become the first Sinn Féin lord mayor of Belfast in 2002–03. On 17 April 2003, Sir John Stevens told a press conference in Belfast: 'I have uncovered enough evidence to lead me to believe that the murders of Patrick Finucane and Brian Adam Lambert could have been prevented. I also believe that the RUC investigation of Patrick Finucane's murder should have resulted in the early arrest and detection of his killers.'

Stevens went on to say that evidence of collusion lay in the wilful failure to keep records, the absence of accountability, the withholding of intelligence and evidence, and through to the extreme measure of agents being involved in murder: 'These serious acts and omissions have meant that people have been killed or seriously injured. The unlawful involvement of agents in murder implies that the security forces sanction killings … nationalists were known to be targeted but were not properly warned or protected. The coordination, dissemination and sharing of intelligence were poor. Informants and agents were allowed to operate without effective control and to participate in terrorist crimes. Crucial information was withheld from senior investigating officers.'

Based on Stevens's reports, accessed by us and confirmed by authoritative sources, we can now detail those who died as a direct, or indirect, result of Nelson's activities. The FRU's role in handling Nelson was ostensibly to ensure 'proper targeting', instead of the UDA simply murdering random Catholics. In fact, as this list will demonstrate, Nelson continued to provide UDA gunmen with the names of Catholics who had no connection with the IRA or any other republican organisation. It is clear that while the FRU provided Nelson with material such as photographs and addresses and other confidential intelligence details to facilitate his targeting of IRA and Sinn Féin members, Brian Nelson used the same operational methods to invent files on ordinary members of the Catholic community to give bogus justification for shooting them. On one occasion he even produced a victim whom he assumed was a Catholic, but turned out to be a Protestant. According to Sir John Stevens in April and November 2003, it seems the FRU did nothing to prevent the murders of such individuals.

Furthermore, even though the FRU would have known that UDA 'teams' had gone out to kill a random Catholic, they did nothing either to stop the murder taking place or to arrest the gunmen.

Edward Campbell, a forty-year-old Catholic taxi driver, is an example of such a random killing. He was abducted and shot by the UDA/UFF on 3 July 1987. Although he had been interned in the 1970s, he had no IRA connections when he was murdered. The north Belfast man's body was found dumped close to a quarry near the Horseshoe Bend in the city.

Patrick Hamill, a twenty-nine-year-old Catholic from Forfar Street in west Belfast, was shot dead at his home on 9 September 1987. Files given to Nelson by the FRU were used by the UDA/UFF for the murder. This was also a purely sectarian murder, as Hamill had no connection with any paramilitary organisation.

Jim Meighan, a twenty-two-year-old Catholic from the New Lodge in north Belfast, was targeted by Nelson because he was going out with a Protestant girl. He was shot dead on 21 September 1987, as he sat in a car with his girlfriend outside Prestwick Park in Ballysillan, Belfast. He had no connection with any paramilitary organisation. At the UDA men's trial the judge said Meighan was killed 'simply because he was an innocent Catholic'.

Francisco Notorantonio, sixty-seven years old, was shot dead as he lay in bed, next to his wife, on the morning of 9 October 1987. (This murder is examined in more detail later in this book.)

Adam Lambert, nineteen, was a Protestant Building Services student at the University of Ulster. He was targeted by Nelson the day after the Enniskillen bombing, which left eleven Protestants dead. UDA men had made two failed murder attempts already that day, and targeted Lambert on the basis of information that Nelson supplied. Nelson believed that Lambert was a Catholic, and the young man was shot dead at a building site in Belfast on 9 November 1987. Nelson's handlers knew he had been involved in the killing, but did nothing about it.

Terence (Terry) McDaid was a twenty-nine-year-old father of two from Newington Street, off north Belfast's Antrim Road. Nelson's target was a relative of McDaid's, but he mistakenly passed the wrong address to the UDA/UFF murder team. McDaid, who had no paramilitary connections, was shot seven times as his children screamed at the top of the stairs. He died on 10 May 1988.

Gerard Slane, twenty-seven, was shot dead at his home in Waterville Street, off the Falls Road, in the early hours of 23 September 1988. A targeting file had been prepared prior to the murder by Nelson, with the help of his FRU handlers. A former republican prisoner, Slane had no political or para-military ties at the time of his death.

Patrick (Pat) Finucane, a thirty-eight-year-old married man with three children, was a Catholic solicitor. He was shot dead in front of his family in the kitchen of their north Belfast home on 12 February 1989. He had no connection with any paramilitary organisation. (This murder is examined in more detail later in this book.)

John Joe Davey was a fifty-eight-year-old veteran republican from Gulladuff, County Derry. He had fought in the IRA's ill-fated border campaign of 1956–1962. Nelson supplied his files to the UDA and the UVF, and to UDA freelance killer Michael Stone. The UVF shot Davey dead as he returned home after a meeting of Magherafelt District Council, of which he was an elected Sinn Féin representative, on the night of 14 February 1989. Stone had tried and failed to kill Davey a year earlier.

Patrick Feeney, thirty-two, was a Catholic who worked as a security man at a linen mill in Donaghcloney, County Tyrone. Brian Nelson targeted Feeney and passed his files to the UDA/UFF. Feeney was shot dead at his place of work on 22 February 1989. This was a purely sectarian murder, as Feeney had no connections with any paramilitary organisation.

Gerard Casey, twenty-nine, was an IRA member who lived in the north Antrim town of Rasharkin. Nelson supplied intelligence documents on Casey to his UDA/UFF colleagues, and on the night of 4 April 1989 two UDA/UFF men burst into the house through a window and shot him dead as he lay in bed with his wife. The IRA claimed at the time that there was RUC and UDR collusion in the murder. A sketch map of the interior of Casey's house had been drawn by police during a raid the previous October.

Liam McKee, a thirty-nine-year-old Catholic from Lisburn, County Antrim, was shot dead at his home in Donard Drive on 24 June 1989. Nelson had supplied information on him to the UDA/UFF, who later claimed responsibility for his murder. McKee had no political or paramilitary connections, even though Nelson's files had listed him as an IRA member.

Loughlin 'Locky' Maginn, a twenty-eight-year-old Catholic from Rathfriland in County Down, was a married man with four children. He had been a victim of harassment by members of the security forces when he was targeted for assassination by Nelson. On 25 August 1989, a UDA/UFF gang fired shots at Maginn through the front window of his home on the Lissize estate and then climbed through the window and shot him dead in the hallway.

Later, Tommy 'Tucker' Lyttle, the UDA's west Belfast commander, tried to justify the killing by releasing a picture of Maginn allegedly taken from a security force montage. The picture had, in fact, been taken by 'showbiz' photographer Billy McCarroll from a television broadcast image and then inserted into a faked montage. (McCarroll, who died in 2002, was subsequently jailed for three years for his role in this cover-up.) Lyttle's bid to 'prove' Maginn was an IRA suspect would, in the end, lead to his own imprisonment. The propaganda exercise backfired spectacularly when Sir John Stevens was called in to investigate allegations of collusion between loyalists and members of the security forces.

As a result of the Stevens investigation into the matter, evidence was gathered concerning Brian Nelson and his central involvement in these crimes, including his role as an agent, leading to a warrant for his arrest. However, when the Stevens Inquiry team went to arrest Brian Nelson on 11 January 1990, the agent was nowhere to be found. His handlers had tipped him off and moved him to England as panic set in inside the FRU amidst fears that their methods of operating would be exposed to scrutiny. Nelson returned ten days later, after handing over his UDA targeting files and computer disks to his handlers. He pleaded guilty to five conspiracy-to-murder charges at his trial on 22 January 1992. The court heard that one of the conspiracy-to-murder charges related to a plot to kill Sinn Féin councillor Alex Maskey as he was dining in The Gregory restaurant on north Belfast's Antrim Road in 1988. A Crown lawyer told the court that Nelson had actively targeted Maskey. The other charges related to Terence McDaid, Gerard Slane and two other incidents which occurred in November 1988 involving aborted attempts on the lives of Patrick Monaghan and James Morgan. Crown counsel Brian Kerr told Belfast Crown Court, 'In each of these cases, Mr Nelson played a vital and indispensable role.' Nelson was jailed in 1992 for ten years for his terrorist offences. At the trial 'Colonel J', then CO of the FRU, in an attempt to exonerate Nelson, claimed the agent had saved 217 lives. In May 2003, Sir John said he found that the FRU was 'responsible for preventing only two killings', although he refrained from naming those who had escaped death. We know that one was Gerry Adams, Sinn Féin president; the second remains unknown. In 1992, after Nelson's trial, the FRU changed its name to the Joint Services Group (JSG).

Amongst those who, by sheer good fortune, survived Nelson's death plots was Alex Maskey, as well as a number of solicitors, including Paddy McGrory and Oliver Kelly. Paddy McGrory, who died of a heart attack in 1994 at the age of seventy-one, was a respected lawyer who served on the council of the Law Society of Northern Ireland and had been appointed by the lord chief justice to a disciplinary tribunal. Like Pat Finucane and Oliver Kelly, McGrory often represented clients on IRA charges, some high-profile, and to some RUC officers this made him an IRA sympathiser. In August 2002, the allegations concerning the targeting of Kelly and McGrory emerged, and Kelly told the *Guardian*: 'This is what the cops were feeding out to loyalists: if you defended someone in court you were acting against the State. They felt that you should throw in the towel; you shouldn't defend someone to the best of your ability. They were telling the loyalists to wipe us [lawyers who defended IRA members] out – to take us out of the road.' McGrory's son, Barra, also a lawyer, said in 2002: 'The inescapable conclusion is that military intelligence wanted the targeting to occur. Uninterrupted. They didn't want anything to stand in its way.' The security forces failed to inform either Kelly or McGrory of the murder plots being planned against them. Asked if he had ever been warned, Kelly said: 'It just didn't happen. But I was hearing from other sources what the cops were saying about us to loyalist-type persons – that we were up to our eyes in the Provos, we were worse than the worst, we were orchestrating things and all that nonsense.'

In July 1989, five months after the murder of Belfast solicitor Pat Finucane, Nelson received a report from a regular UFF informant containing details about a suitable place to shoot McGrory. He passed this report on to his FRU handlers. The Stevens Inquiry has recovered this targeting document. It notes that McGrory spent 'a lot of time' in the Chester bar on Belfast's Antrim Road, and that he went there 'in the late afternoon', and that every Sunday he visited the Kitchen bar, driving there in his Mercedes, which he parked 'unprotected' nearby. Stevens would conclude that the security forces were reckless in failing to warn McGrory – and would have been complicit in his murder had it gone ahead.

Soon after he was jailed, Brian Nelson was moved to England to serve the rest of his ten-year sentence. He served just four years before being released and immediately disappeared off the radar. Ministry of Defence sources placed him variously in Canada, Northumbria and New Zealand. When his death was announced in April 2003, the MOD said he had died in Canada. In September 2003 an investigation by the *Belfast Telegraph*'s Chris Thornton finally uncovered the truth: Nelson – now 'Brian Thompson' – had died of lung cancer in Cardiff, Wales, at the age of fifty-six. Thornton had obtained a copy of Nelson's death certificate during the course of his investigation which verified that his death had been officially registered by his family and certified by the Cardiff GP who had treated him during his battle with cancer. The Army agent's assumed name was given by his eldest son, who was recorded as being present when Nelson died. But his birthdate – 30 September 1947 – was genuine, as was his place of birth. Nelson's occupation was listed as 'Army Officer (retired)'. This, we felt, was confirmation of our belief that Brian Nelson had never left the British Army, but had remained on the payroll since the 1960s when he had first joined the Black Watch.

Arming the Loyalists – *Ingram*

At the time I knew it was wrong. Ever since, the actions of some of my colleagues in the Force Research Unit – such as the decision to arm loyalists and to pay for weapons to be imported into Northern Ireland – have been the cause of many sleepless nights for me. The thinking of the FRU at that time was not dissimilar to that of recent regimes in Colombia, where right-wing paramilitary death squads were armed and run by the State. In the 1980s the FRU believed, wrongly, that it was its responsibility to redress the balance after republicans were supplied with arms from Libya, and that the most effective way to carry out that responsibility was to use loyalists to take the fight to the republicans. The FRU was using loyalist paramilitaries as an extension of the British Army.

In conversations I had with other FRU officers – obviously we all discussed our cases with each other and were knowledgeable of the 'bigger picture' – it became evident that the organisation was intimately involved in both the procurement and the distribution of arms obtained with the knowledge of both Armscor, the South African armaments body, and the South African government. (Prior to this, weapons were either home-made or stolen, but after the Libyan arms running, loyalists felt compelled to approach a more dependable source. The right-wing South African State of the time proved compatible to their needs.) The FRU officers involved in these operations did not consider arming an illegal paramilitary organisation to be wrong; the thinking was that 'the end justifies the means', the 'end' being the rooting out of republicanism at its core. A senior FRU officer personally told me that the importation of arms had two main advantages: firstly, the acquisition of automatic weapons and hand grenades increased the operational capability of the UDA, and secondly, it improved the standing and prestige that Brian Nelson enjoyed within the UDA, which in turn meant more influence and a larger degree of control over the paramilitaries by the FRU, through their agent.

As is clear from these pages, I am no fan of the RUC, but in this case I cannot lay the blame for these activities at its door.

A fellow FRU officer told me that the RUC was not cognisant of the deal, which makes sense because, based on my experience, I believe the RUC would not have allowed such an operation to proceed for one particular reason: the growing access and influence within loyalist circles that Brian Nelson gave the Army and, more to the point, the FRU. The RUC was already resentful of the FRU running an agent within loyalism, which was meant to be the RUC's exclusive domain. Nelson had slipped through the net because he was either a former British soldier or an AWOL soldier who had never technically left the Army – as an employee or ex-employee of the Army, he legitimately fell under the FRU's jurisdiction.

Finance for the arms was organised through illegal activities – bank robberies, extortion, etc – with the tacit understanding and compliance of the FRU. Once purchased, the imported weapons were tracked from source to distribution by the FRU and MI5 by electronic means. This means that MI5 were aware of the activities, which means, by implication, that the politicians were too, as it was the duty of MI5 to keep politicians informed of major developments on the ground in Northern Ireland – and these were clearly major developments.

Brian Nelson was the loyalist representative in the negotiations to procure these weapons, which were then distributed between the three loyalist groups: the UDA, the UVF and Ulster Resistance. The FRU would later inform the RUC of two of these weapons hauls in Northern Ireland, but allowed a third one – including more than 100 rifles and pistols – to go to loyalist paramilitaries. This was an outrageous breach of democratic principles, but to those involved at the

FRU end, such principles didn't matter. As well as facilitating weapons shipments into Northern Ireland, Nelson was allowed to come and go as he pleased. He personally delivered Armscor manuals to the home of the UDA's west Belfast boss Tommy 'Tucker' Lyttle, himself an RUC Special Branch informant. Lyttle would pick and choose which weapons he wanted before giving his orders to Nelson. Each time, Brian Nelson met with both South African and MI5 representatives in London before flying to Johannesburg and the arms dealers. He was given 'safe passage' through customs to South Africa and back to Belfast on at least five occasions.

Douglas Bernhardt, an American-born agent for BOSS, the South African government's secret intelligence agency, put loyalists in touch with a Lebanese gunrunner, Joe Fawzi, in 1987. The UDA, UVF and Ulster Resistance paid Fawzi around stg£400,000 (stolen in a bank robbery in Portadown that was allowed to proceed by the FRU) for a large consignment of weapons, including hundreds of AK47s which had fallen into the hands of Lebanese Christian militias, captured from the retreating PLO when it was expelled from south Lebanon in 1982. And so, with the indirect help of South African agents and the complicity of the FRU and M15, the UDA and the UVF were able to intensify their violence up until the 1994 ceasefire. There can be little doubt that even with the 'interception' of those two arms shipments by the RUC, a large number of these arms are still in existence and presumably still pose a threat.

Chapter 10

The Murder of Pat Finucane

Harkin

Pat Finucane was a dedicated lawyer, a husband and a father, but he was also a wanted man, a hate figure for many members of the Royal Ulster Constabulary, and he knew it. Clients finally given access to him after being detained by the police – a routine occurrence – would warn him of what detectives had said during their period of custody: he would 'be got'. Pat Finucane believed in the law and he believed in using the law to the best advantage of his clients, regardless of who or what they were. Unfortunately for Finucane, many of his clients were republicans. There were people in the RUC, right up to the highest levels, who could not distinguish between Finucane's fundamental duty to represent and defend his clients and the beliefs and actions of those clients. In security circles he became 'the enemy', tarred with the same brush as the republicans he represented in court. But while the thought that there were those in the RUC and the UDA who wanted Finucane dead is disturbing, what makes his murder most alarming is the role played by the security forces and their agents.

The events leading to Finucane's murder began late in 1988 when Sir Jack Hermon, then RUC chief constable, along with two senior RUC officers, gave a briefing to

Conservative Home Office Minister Douglas Hogg in Belfast. During this private discussion, which is now a matter of public record, Hermon told the minister that solicitors working in Northern Ireland were helping known paramilitaries to beat terror raps. When, a few weeks later, on 17 January 1989, Hogg rose to speak in the House of Commons during a Prevention of Terrorism Act debate, he stated that some lawyers in Northern Ireland were 'unduly sympathetic to the IRA'. Hermon later said that he was furious with Hogg for this breach of confidence, and the minister was criticised by politicians and lawyers alike for his comments. He could not have known the effect of those words: he had unwittingly put in motion a chain of events that would end in the murder of Mr Finucane.

Since then, much has been made of what Douglas Hogg said during that House of Commons debate. In his interim report on the murder, Sir John Stevens said his inquiry team had investigated these allegations. He told reporters: 'Mr Hogg's comments ... aroused controversy. To the extent that they were based on information passed by the RUC, they were not justifiable and the inquiry concludes that the minister was compromised.' Stevens was therefore accusing former RUC chief constable Sir Jack Hermon, who had told Hogg specifically that Patrick Finucane was aiding the IRA, of compromising, or misleading a government minister.

Sir Jack Hermon may have been furious with Hogg for repeating in public information given to him confidentially, but it didn't stop him repeating his claims about Finucane ten years later, in 1999, in an interview with the *Sunday Times*. Hermon claimed that Finucane had been associated with the IRA and had used his position as a lawyer to 'act as a contact between suspects in custody and republicans on the outside'. He went on to say that Hogg's comments represented 'a statement based on fact'. But at the inquest into the murdered solicitor's death in 1990, an RUC officer said: 'The police refute the claim that Mr Finucane was a member of PIRA. He was just another law-abiding citizen going about his professional duties in a professional manner.' The Stevens Inquiry concluded that Finucane was not a member of any paramilitary group, and found Mr Hogg's claims totally unjustified.

But all of this came too late for Pat Finucane and his family. UDA west Belfast commander Tommy 'Tucker' Lyttle told me that within hours of Hogg's speech in the Commons on 17 January, he, Lyttle, met with his Special Branch handler. Despite his reign of terror in the city, Lyttle continued to work for the security forces – an incredible situation in any democracy. Lyttle later claimed that his handler discussed Hogg's comments with him and said, 'Why don't you whack Finucane?' Brian Nelson was then summoned to Lyttle's home in Sydney Street West and told to prepare an intelligence file on the lawyer. What Lyttle didn't know was that Brian Nelson was already actively targeting Pat Finucane. At least two warnings about this activity had appeared in FRU reports and had been passed to MI5 and RUC Special Branch, but, incredibly, none of these warnings had been passed on to Finucane. Lyttle also later met with Eric McKee, a notorious loyalist killer, and Jim Spence, a UFF terror commander who was also working as an agent for Special Branch. They discussed the possibility of killing Finucane.

When Nelson reported back to his handlers that Lyttle had requested a file on Finucane, FRU officers actively encouraged him and gave him every possible assistance. This was, at the time, a standard FRU response – to help its agent compile accurate reports for his UDA bosses, which in turn secured his standing in the organisation and strengthened their position. The FRU usually passed on warnings about what it knew of the imminent operation to Special Branch. Accordingly, the FRU provided Nelson with photographs and detailed maps of Finucane's home, located off the city's Antrim Road. Even more questionable was the fact that handlers were also involved in reconnaissance missions at the Finucane family home. There was at least one occasion when a FRU officer drove Brian Nelson to Fortwillam Drive to see the Finucanes' house. Another time, a FRU officer posed as a window cleaner with Nelson and they offered their 'services' to a neighbour of the Finucanes so they could check out the rear of their target's home.

It is inconceivable that by this stage senior RUC Special Branch officers and senior members of the FRU did not know that Pat Finucane was a definite UDA target. Special Branch, in particular, could have acted to prevent the murder, as almost every single UDA/UFF operative involved in the murder plot was an agent/informer for the organisation, including old hands William Stobie and Tommy 'Tucker' Lyttle.

The murder plot was simple. A hit squad of three, one driver and two shooters, was assembled and issued with guns. The three – Ken Barrett, 'M' and 'X' – made their way to the Finucane house one grey Sunday evening, 12 February 1989. When Barrett and his UFF terror colleagues burst into the house at 7.30pm, the lawyer was eating a late Sunday dinner with his wife and three children. He didn't stand a chance. Finucane was shot fourteen times and died instantly on the floor of his kitchen, in front of his family.

Just weeks before he was murdered by the UDA on 12 December 2001, William Stobie met with me and claimed that he hadn't known who was being targeted that fateful day – 12 February 1989. We met in a Belfast city-centre café and discussed the case, as we had done many times before, and as always he denied knowing that Finucane was the target. I didn't believe him entirely. I believe that, at the very least, the gunmen who came to pick up the weapons for the shooting would have mentioned the forthcoming operation to Stobie. I believe he may have been told that a solicitor was going to be shot, but when pressed, Stobie again denied this. Members of the Finucane family have always felt he was holding back vital information.

Whatever he did or did not know, Stobie did what he always did when UDA/UFF hitmen came looking for guns – he called his handlers. On the evening Pat Finucane died, Stobie wasn't the only Special Branch agent calling a handler. According to a loyalist source I spoke with, UFF boss Jim Spence was also making phone calls to his handler in the Branch to see if the coast was clear for the hit team to move across town and attack Finucane. He was assured of safe passage.

Stobie was clear in his own mind about what had happened on the afternoon and early evening of 12 February. We met in a bar in County Down a week before his murder, and he gave me details on condition I would not publish them until it was cleared by his solicitor, Joe Rice. I agreed.

Stobie told me that he got a phone call and was told to bring some 'gear' to a club on the Highfield estate in west

Belfast. Ken Barrett, 'M' and 'X' were waiting for him there. When Stobie arrived, he recalled, Barrett complained because he had brought a Heckler and Koch machine pistol while Barrett had wanted a 9mm Browning; the Heckler and Koch held only nine bullets while the Browning held thirteen rounds, twelve in the magazine and one in the barrel. It was decided that Barrett and M would do the shooting while X would drive. Stobie claimed that X didn't know who the target was either, and didn't even know there was going to be a shooting until he heard the shots crack out from the Finucane home – he had been told that it was just a reconnaissance mission. Jim Spence, the UFF unit commander who saw the team off, assured the gunmen that they had been guaranteed safe passage to and from the scene of the crime by his police friends – his RUC Special Branch handlers.

Stobie described the scene to me as follows: 'I gave them [the hit team] the guns. Spence said it was for a special job, that a top Provie was going to be hit. I left the club, got to a phone and told my handler. I said who was in the club and what they wanted. I later saw them [the hit team] get into a van and knew they were off. I called my handler again and they said they would look into it. I told them what guns they had. These guns had been taken away by my handlers before, so they knew which ones I was talking about.' I asked Stobie if the weapons had been 'jarked', that is, fitted with bugs or tracking devices. He replied: 'I don't know about that, but they [my handlers] had always checked all the weapons I kept for the UDA.' We were finishing up our meeting when Stobie stopped for a second and added: 'I did tell you, didn't I, that there was an Army helicopter up over Highfield that Sunday, from the moment those boys got the guns.' This was typical of Stobie, giving you important information nonchalantly. We finished up our meeting and prepared to leave – Stobie had told me all he could.

Did Stobie know more about the Finucane case that could do damage to loyalism or the security forces? I don't believe he did. And he obviously felt his knowledge was useless, or at least of limited use, because he believed he was safe. He continued to live in Belfast, openly – and vulnerably – going about his day-to-day business. In May 1994 he was abducted in the Lower Shankill area of west Belfast and shot four times and injured by Johnny Adair of the UFF in an alleyway just off the Shankill Road in west Belfast. The attack was reported in newspapers at the time as a punishment shooting, but Stobie believed differently, telling me: 'Adair left me for dead in that entry, there's no doubt about that. It was an attempt to murder me, not punish me, but I survived, recovered and was told later [by Adair] I had been punished for being a tout [traitor] and that was the end of it. I was told to stay away from certain people and certain premises and that was it. I thought afterwards that this was not just about Adair, this was about the Branch or someone like that telling me to keep my mouth shut about Finucane – well, not telling me, I suppose, 'cos they thought they had shut my trap permanently.'

In June 1999 Stobie was arrested and charged in connection with Finucane's murder. The sole evidence against him was a statement given to police by the former journalist and ex-Northern Ireland Office press officer Neil Mulholland, who had interviewed Stobie off the record more than ten years earlier. Neil Mulholland was a fantastic journalist (he no longer works in media), who went after the big stories when others were happy regurgitating press releases. He had met with Stobie in the late 1980s, and Stobie had discussed the Finucane murder with him. Neil decided against running the story, but gave the details to fellow journalist Ed Moloney. Moloney was later questioned about Stobie, but he refused to hand over his notes or to give evidence against Stobie. At this point, Neil Mulholland decided to make a statement to the Stevens Inquiry about Stobie's claim that he had supplied the murder weapons. This, in turn, led to Stobie's arrest. Throughout the trial, Neil was very unwell and he eventually indicated that he no longer wished to give evidence against Stobie. The situation in which Neil found himself was intolerable and, whatever the debate over the morals of giving the statement in the first place, he suffered for it. He was a 'victim' of the fall-out from the Stevens Inquiry, losing his job and his reputation in the aftermath of the investigations.

In November 2001 Billy Stobie walked free from Belfast Crown Court when the case against him collapsed. Eager to enjoy his new freedom, Stobie had no idea he had only weeks left to live.

I met Stobie again soon after his release, but by then the damage had been done. He had done two television interviews, one for Channel Four and one for UTV's 'Insight' programme. In both interviews he backed calls from the Finucane family for a full independent inquiry into the murder. This may seem a strange move on Stobie's part, but he felt victimised by the Stevens Inquiry and was angry that he was the only person every charged in relation to Finucane's murder. He had made a statement alleging that he had told his RUC handlers about the murder plot on the night it was taking place, and he felt let down when it became apparent that no RUC officers would be questioned or arrested. He had, he felt, kept his side of the bargain with his RUC handlers, yet he was the one taking the blame. Whatever his personal motivation, as the suspected gunmen were still active in loyalism, this was a foolish thing to do. I told Stobie so, but he actually believed an assurance given to him by the UDA/UFF that he would not be harmed. I told him he should leave the country, but Billy wouldn't hear of it. He and his girlfriend led a quiet, simple existence, he said, and no one would bother him now that the case had been dropped. He was wrong.

I should say here that Stobie never received payment during any of our meetings, and he never asked for payment – whatever his motivation in talking to me, it wasn't money. Before we parted at this last meeting, I told him to look after himself. A week later, on 12 December 2001, he was dead, gunned down in cold blood at 6.30am by a lone gunman as he left his flat in Forthriver. His simple existence with his girlfriend, his 'little life' as he referred to it, was over. His death was a scandal for both the RUC and the Stevens Inquiry team. It should never have happened.

✳ ✳ ✳

There was another senior UDA official working for Special Branch the weekend that Pat Finucane was murdered – Tommy 'Tucker' Lyttle. Lyttle's involvement is an important aspect of the Finucane murder conspiracy, one that has, for whatever reason, been largely ignored by the Stevens Inquiry and by those who have been spoon-fed 'official' information down the years.

Tucker Lyttle was an intimidating character in loyalist west Belfast, but he was also a source for a number of journalists, including me. In January 1990, eleven months after the murder of Pat Finucane, he phoned and asked me to visit him at his home off the Crumlin Road. He wanted to give me a story for my paper at the time, the *Sunday News* – a story that wasn't to be published until he gave the go-ahead. When I got there he told me that Brian Nelson was his intelligence officer in the UDA and that he knew Nelson was also a security force agent. Lyttle produced South African arms manuals and pointed to weapons Nelson had brought into Northern Ireland with the blessing of his handlers. 'We all have our police and Army friends,' said Lyttle. 'I've got mine. But Brian's got the very best of friends.' He predicted Nelson's arrest and then said that there was 'something big going down' in relation to Pat Finucane's murder.

I felt uncomfortable because Tucker was being far more forthcoming than usual. Normally his wife would make tea and leave us in the kitchen where we'd talk for a minute or two about some issue and then I'd leave. This time he was more chatty than he had ever been before. The police and the Army had wanted Finucane dead, he told me, and the UFF were 'happy to oblige'. Lyttle's reason for calling me was simple: he expected to be arrested too and he wanted to issue a warning that if he were charged in relation to the murder of Finucane, he would 'blow this whole thing wide open'. There was more to this than people thought, he said, and he knew exactly what had happened. We arranged to meet again, although as I left his house Lyttle said, 'If it's in the Crum [Crumlin Road prison], I'll arrange a pass.' A few days later Lyttle was arrested and charged with possessing information likely to be useful to terrorists. He was released on bail thirteen days later and was quick to arrange another meeting with me.

That Saturday evening we met at his Sydney Street West home and he told me that Nelson had been arrested and that I should report the fact that he was one of Britain's top agents inside loyalism. Lyttle repeated the arms plot allegations, along with the claim that Nelson, a security force agent supposedly paid to save lives, had set up the murder of one of Northern Ireland's most prominent lawyers. Lyttle told me that, incredibly, all the UDA members involved in the killing attended a 'celebration' party held in his house after the murder. FRU informer Brian Nelson, Special Branch informer Jim Spence and Ken Barrett were among the guests at this macabre gathering.

Like Lyttle, Brian Nelson was also arrested by the Stevens Inquiry, which was investigating allegations of collusion between security forces and loyalist paramilitaries. The two men were questioned about the murder of Pat Finucane, but neither was charged in relation to it. Nonetheless, the whispers of collusion continued, and I investigated deeper into the matter.

In 2000, I discovered from a senior police source that UDA hitman Ken Barrett had confessed to the murder during a conversation with RUC CID officer Johnston Brown in 1991, and that a tape had been made of the confession, without Barrett's knowledge. This tape later disappeared, as I reported in the *People* on 29 April 2001, and was replaced by a tape of a second secretly recorded conversation between Brown and Barrett. This second tape, labelled to look like the original tape, did not include Barrett's murder confession, in which he cruelly described the dead lawyer as 'Fork Finucane' – Finucane was still holding the fork with which he had been eating his dinner when the UFF murder team burst into his house. UTV's 'Insight' programme carried an interview with Officer Johnston Brown two weeks later, in May 2001, confirming my story. It was devastating for the RUC, as it suggested that senior officers had attempted to cover-up an investigation conducted by one of their own team.

Brown claimed that when he gave his statement to the Stevens Inquiry team, they had become agitated by the allegation. This was because the Stevens team had been given the *second* tape by the RUC rather than the first tape, and therefore didn't believe what Brown was saying about his conversation with Barrett. However, after they had listened to the second tape, the Stevens team did believe Brown because on that second tape Barrett was heard discussing a shooting that had taken place *after* the date that was labelled on the tape, ie, a murder attempt was discussed that had taken place five days after this tape was supposed to have been recorded. Even more convincingly, the shooting incident mentioned on the second tape took place after the date Brown had claimed he had first heard Barrett confess to his part in the murder. Johnston Brown realised then that the Stevens team had been given a recording of a second conversation that he had conducted with Barrett, and that this had been swapped with the one he wanted them to hear in which Barrett openly confessed to murdering Pat Finucane. The RUC has now confirmed to the Stevens Inquiry that a first tape did exist, but that they cannot now find it.

In 2002 the BBC's 'Panorama' programme followed this lead and secretly recorded their own 'interviews' with Ken

Barrett, in which he confessed to his part in the killing as well as claiming that he had met Jim Spence's 'friend' in the RUC. He said this officer told him: 'Pat [Finucane] was ... an IRA man, like, he was dealing with finances and stuff for them ... and if he was out [dead], like, they would have a lot of trouble replacing him ... He [the RUC officer] says [to Barrett]: "He'll [Finucane] have to go. He'll have to go." He said, "He's a thorn in everybody's side."'

The last time Ken Barrett was arrested and questioned about the killing of Pat Finucane was in June 1999. When Stevens officers, accompanied by local police, arrived at his home at six o'clock one morning, Barrett was already up, breakfasted and dressed in a suit. Jim Spence was also waiting for officers when they arrived at his home at the same hour. Both men had been tipped off by Special Branch. The two men were released without charge within seventy-two hours of their arrests. Barrett later fled to England after death threats from members of the UDA who believed he had been an RUC informer. Whilst in England the Stevens Inquiry offered him a safe house, which he accepted, but he refused to become involved in a witness protection scheme.

Following on from this refusal to cooperate, the Stevens Inquiry decided to target Barrett in a Sting Operation. Detectives knew Barrett had a habit of chatting openly about his exploits (for example, to Brown in 1991 and to BBC reporter John Ware in 2002), so members of the Stevens team posed as criminals and set the tapes recording as Barrett, once again, confessed to killing Pat Finucane. At the time of writing, Ken Barrett is on remand in prison charged with Finucane's murder, based on the evidence of two separate undercover Stevens Inquiry operations.

In April 2003, Stevens found that the murder of Pat Finucane was 'wholly preventable'. I believe the murder of Pat
Finucane was not only preventable but was actively allowed
to take place. The solicitor hadn't been warned about the
threats to his life, even though members of the security forces
and their agents were involved in the planning, targeting
and execution of the killing. MI5, the political overseers,
were aware of the targeting of Finucane, but did nothing.
Subsequent investigations into his death were hindered by
cover-up after cover-up.

Martin Ingram will argue later in this book that while the
FRU did target Finucane, it passed on all information gathered to the RUC and it was up to the RUC to act upon that
information. This is true. Ninety percent of the blame for the
murder rests with the RUC and, in particular, with Special
Branch. William Stobie and two of the puppet-masters,
Tommy Lyttle and Jim Spence, were Special Branch agents.
Both gunmen, Ken Barrett and 'M', would go on to work as
paid police agents; it almost beggars belief. However, I
believe the FRU cannot wash the blood off its hands in this
murder. It assisted Brian Nelson, a man it knew to be a multiple murderer, in targeting Finucane. Little wonder then that
the Finucane family demands answers.

Pat Finucane's widow, Geraldine, her children and Peter
Madden, Finucane's business partner, continue to argue for a
public inquiry into the murder. It is hoped that a recommendation for such an inquiry will be forthcoming. In comments
to the author in May 2003, Peter Madden said: 'The campaign
will continue. The family will continue to seek support. They
have waited long enough for the truth. Pat Finucane, in his
short career, sought justice for a large number of people. He

was too successful. I have to play my part in seeking justice for him. I owe him that at least.' In 2001 I arranged for Peter Madden to meet FRU whistleblower Martin Ingram, so that Ingram could tell him what he knew about the killing.

Despite repeated calls for a public inquiry into the death of Patrick Finucane, neither the British nor the Irish government has taken steps to accommodate such an inquiry. Perhaps it will be that the facts of the murder of Patrick Finucane will never be known, and those responsible may never be brought to justice.

Chapter 11

Collusion and Conspiracy

Ingram

The atmosphere and direction of the FRU during the late 1980s, in contrast to my first tour in the early 1980s, was stark and uncompromising. The principal reason, I believe, for this change was the appointment of an ambitious new senior officer. I knew my new superior well; indeed, I think I can safely say that he was the best commanding officer that I had ever worked for. He was bright, witty, articulate and at times charming. I will admit I liked him not only as my boss but also as a person.

Traditionally, the system of the FRU was built on results achieved by acceptable means, within recognised parameters. However, during the mid- to late 1980s this system was undermined and a more aggressive and liberal interpretation of 'acceptable means' came into play. In this new climate, officers were keen – and able – to explore areas that had previously been off-limits to them – limits like the crossing of an international border into the Republic on duty; limits like encouraging handlers to stretch the bounds of normal practice.

That said, consider this: when running an agent in a 'sensitive' role, for example, Brian Nelson's role as intelligence officer in the UDA, it is impossible to remain within the strict bounds of the law, and at times might even be detrimental or indeed dangerous to do so. There are moral grey areas and tough decisions must be made. To that extent, no one officer, regardless of rank, deserves to be saddled with all the responsibility. The Army is no different from many other employers. Results are required to move forward, whether it is to satisfy a local boss, to further a career or merely for personal satisfaction. In the real world each and every handler knew that they would be judged by one thing: results. We had many customers to satisfy, all pressing for both strategic (ie, long-term) and tactical (ie, day-to-day or instantly exploitable) intelligence. The commander land forces (CLF) and the commanding officers of SIW, MI5 and the RUC were some of our clients. They were insatiable in their hunger for exploitable intelligence to aid their efforts to prevent loss of life and frustrate the enemy.

The FRU was a special and separate unit and those in command of that unit enjoyed privileges not open to other senior Army officers, such as a massive budget, well-trained and motivated soldiers, freedom to operate outside the structures which report directly to the RUC. This sort of freedom could be exploited and, on rare occasions, abused. It depended on the individual. Some individuals, in my opinion, did abuse this responsibility. This FRU posting had everything an ambitious, career-minded officer could have wanted – and it attracted exactly that kind of person. To many, it sounded too good to be true, and in some ways it was, because there was a risk in allowing any officer so much room for manoeuvre. There should have been safeguards in place, a series of checks and balances which would have constrained individual officers. It is too late now, but our legislators let everyone down by allowing the FRU to operate in Northern Ireland with no written terms of reference or guidelines other than Common Law.

Obviously there is a hierarchy above and beyond the FRU, but that did not, nor could it, impinge on the day-to-day operations of the Unit. I, for one, never received any advice or instructions from anyone or any organisation outside the FRU. Our operations and activities may have been reported to ministers, including prime ministers, in regular briefings, but that is not to say that they had anything other than a general understanding of the overall intelligence picture. A military intelligence source report (MISR), which was what the FRU produced for the political establishment, is a sanitised version of a contact form (CF – a record of every contact with an agent). A person reading a MISR would have no knowledge of the identity of the agent in question nor of the methods employed to compile that report. The material that a minister received was brief and to the point, with salient points delineated. In no way was it explained how the intelligence in the report was collected; it merely served to inform the reader. At meetings I have attended where senior people were being briefed on aspects of intelligence-gathering, standard need-to-know criteria were always strictly enforced – in a nutshell, someone who doesn't need to know the identity of an agent would not be told, even if they asked.

This means, in effect, that the FRU was a self-regulating body. The commanding officer of the FRU had the power to authorise any operation as he, or she, saw fit, based on the intelligence collected by the operatives. It is therefore easy to see how things could get out of hand, as I believe they did in this period.

I should say further that I make no suggestion that those in the higher echelons of the military, or political system colluded in any plots to murder or physically attack any individual. Any mistakes that were made – and they were made, not only in the Finucane case but in many others – were down to one thing: the FRU. That said, the role of MI5 is worthy of inspection. A representative of the security service shared office space with the FRU operations officer, and was privy to all materials. It was common when discussing possible exploitation of material that the conversation would include input from MI5. It is certain that ministers were also kept informed by the security service of the ongoing case files on agents, although great care would have been taken to ensure there was no paper trail, or indeed smoking gun, in the hands of any minister.

The level of self-regulation enjoyed by the FRU was dented when the Stevens Inquiry was established. The FRU was now expected to cooperate in terms of making an honest disclosure – something that was unprecedented in its history. The Army initially told the Stevens Inquiry that they ran no agents in Northern Ireland. However, the British police investigating the Unit quickly established that a network of over one hundred agents was already in place and had been for over twenty years. The level of cooperation received by Sir John Stevens in the first six months of the inquiry into collusion was virtually nil, and the general perception of the handlers was that the police would not be granted permission to view any file connected with an agent. Even when some documents were eventually handed over to the team, they were not complete, or, to be more accurate, they had been 'refined'. To my knowledge, many original documents were never supplied and it was some eleven years later before the inquiry received the registry books, which point to the existence of many of the missing documents.

❋ ❋ ❋

Some FRU members involved in the Brian Nelson case, including some currently serving as PSNI officers, have appeared on national television to reveal their roles in conspiracies to murder. None, to my knowledge, has accepted that what they did then was wrong, and none seem to appreciate that to frustrate genuine inquiries by police officers to establish the truth is also wrong. To those who are unclear as to what constitutes 'collusion', the Collins dictionary defines it as 'a secret agreement for fraudulent purpose'. I contend that if you help a terrorist to further the targeting of a victim, or if you fail to utilise knowledge in your possession to prevent the loss of life, then you are guilty of collusion. Furthermore, anyone who stands in the way of a properly constituted criminal inquiry should be viewed as a criminal.

I am of the firm opinion that collusion was occurring during this period. In that respect, the murder of Pat Finucane was a defining moment for the FRU and for the Troubles as a whole. I believe that at least one of the handlers involved in the Pat Finucane case sensed the trouble that was looming, although that handler confirmed to me on more than one occasion that they were comfortable with their role in the events. That said, I did have conversations at the time outlining my concerns with a number of senior officers and others more directly involved in the case. Some of those conversations got quite animated. As a result of one such discussion, in late 1989, my superior officer made the following remark in my confidential personnel report: '... that he [Ingram] does need to ensure that his views are articulated in a moderate and balanced manner ...'

A large number of FRU handlers, myself included, were aware of Brian Nelson's activities, in particular, during the late 1980s, and a number of us felt the situation was escalating to a point where, sooner or later, it would end in tears. There was a level of anxiety in the Unit regarding the direction in which Nelson was being steered, and, by implication, the way in which the FRU was being managed. Sadly, not one person, myself included, felt sufficiently outraged to take a stand. It is only in recent years, many years after the events, that I have felt I ought to speak out. In truth, a small part of me wonders to this day if any of what was to come could have been averted if I, or we, had taken a more proactive stance.

Chapter 12

Notorantonio: The Watershed

Harkin

In August and September of 1987, Tommy 'Tucker' Lyttle, the west Belfast commander of the UDA/UFF, asked his intelligence officer, Brian Nelson, for details on top Provisional IRA members. When Brian Nelson supplied 'details', it usually meant bad news for the subject of his file. Among the names Lyttle requested information on was the deputy head of the IRA's Nutting Squad, Frederick Scappaticci. Nelson informed his handlers at FRU of the names on the hit-list, but he had no idea of the panic triggered by the name 'Scappaticci'. Nelson did not know that Scappaticci was working for the exact same unit that he himself served. He did not know that Scappaticci was a highly valued agent who had infiltrated the IRA at its highest levels. He did not know that this man was 'Stakeknife'.

The FRU had to work fast to avoid losing one of its best agents. One of Nelson's handlers convinced him to hold off, promising that a 'good' target would be selected for him, one that would go down well with the UDA in west Belfast. That bought some time, and eventually Nelson was provided with details on Francisco Notorantonio, a pensioner who lived in Ballymurphy in west Belfast. The FRU handler convinced Nelson that Notorantonio was the godfather of the

IRA in Ballymurphy – right in the middle of Gerry Adams's home territory – the head of the Italian-Irish IRA gang, as the handler put it. The profile fit: the Italian name, an old republican who had been interned in the 1940s and the 1970s and who had just recently retired from driving a Falls Road black taxi. Nelson took the bait, and so did Tucker Lyttle.

The next step was intelligence-gathering on the elderly Notorantonio. In late September, British Army soldiers burst through the front door of the Notorantonios' house and into their home. During the raid, soldiers drew diagrams of both the upstairs and the downstairs layout of the house. They went from room to room, noting the design or colour of wallpaper, the furniture and layout, asking the family who occupied each bedroom upstairs. These diagrams were then passed on to the FRU. 'It was standard procedure [during a raid] at the time,' said Charlotte, Francisco Notorantonio's daughter, 'but all they were interested in during that raid was who slept where. My parents could see from the diagram that other details were included, things like the colour of the walls, things like that. I believe this was later used in the murder. The gunmen [the UDA/UFF hitmen who murdered her father] did drop a British Army map as they left and it was a map of Ballymurphy, Whitecliffe Parade and my parents' home. I remember it was given to Sinn Féin to highlight collusion in the case, but we don't know where that map is now.'

Lyttle despatched his death squad to the home of the Notorantonios in Whitecliffe Parade just before 7.30am on 9 October 1987. When the two UFF gunmen burst into the house, they went upstairs and straight into the bedroom the father of eleven shared with his wife of thirty-eight years,

Edith. She told me recently: 'I have very bad hearing, so I didn't hear the front door being kicked in, but Francisco must have because he woke me up as he tried to sit up in bed. I thought it was a British Army raid of some sort. We had been raided a few times and I expected to see a soldier at the bedroom door, but instead it was a man wearing a mask. He shot at Francisco, hitting him in the chest and again as he fell he was shot in the back. I shouted, 'Who are you?' to the gunman, but he didn't say anything. He turned away and then I heard more shots. I looked at Francisco and he wasn't moving. He had been ill anyway and had been waiting on an operation. He hadn't been out of the house in a long time because of his illness. They murdered a very sick man who hadn't been involved in anything in years.'

The dead man's grandson, sixteen-year-old Francisco O'Brien, who was sleeping in another bedroom, hid his face with his hands as a gunman walked in and fired two shots. They both missed. This does not appear to have been an attempt to kill, just a sick act by a gunman who got kicks out of frightening a young boy.

In an interview with the author in 2003, Edith Notorantonio remarked pointedly, 'The day before he was killed, the streets around Ballymurphy were crawling with Brits and the morning he was shot they were nowhere to be seen.' At the time of the murder, Sinn Féin president Gerry Adams, whose father was a close friend of the veteran republican, had echoed her view, saying, 'He was obviously a soft target. I find it very strange that this area was crawling with Crown forces yesterday. They swamped the place. Yet today there was no one around, and armed men were able to come in and out of the area.'

The loyalist hit squad that murdered Francisco Notorantonio — all known to the security forces — celebrated the
murder at a party at Tucker Lyttle's home in Sydney Street
West the day after the killing. Lyttle said he'd held a similar
party following the murder of Pat Finucane, whose personal
details, like Notorantonio's, were supplied by FRU agent,
Brian Nelson. There is no doubt that Lyttle knew about both
killings in advance. The question remains as to whether or
not he warned his Special Branch handlers in advance. The
only way to answer that is to question his handlers directly,
and to ask the RUC for their files from the time, if they still
exist.

Nelson was delighted with the Notorantonio hit, especially when, after Requiem Mass three days later, the pensioner's tricolour-draped coffin was carried from the church
by senior Sinn Féin members, including Gerry Adams and
Tom Hartley. The sight of these high-profile pallbearers lent
weight to the UDA's belief that they had murdered a prominent republican. Among the mourners was Freddie Scappaticci, unaware that the coffin he was following contained the
body of a man who had died to save his life.

✳ ✳ ✳

On Tuesday, 19 September 2000, two men in civilian clothes
walked into the London office of Neil Wallis, UK editor of the
People. They politely asked his secretary to leave and invited
Wallis to sit down. He was handed a number of documents
and told that under no circumstances was he to discuss them
with anyone – not even with me, his news reporter. The representatives were from the Treasury Solicitor (UK State
Solicitor) and the Ministry of Defence and the documents

were injunctions: the first banned the *People* from writing articles on the security forces (the injunction was that wide), the second, more unbelievable still, banned us from reporting the fact that we had been the subject of an injunction! Wallis remarked afterwards, when most of the legal action had been overturned, 'I've never seen anything like it in all my life. It was incredible.'

The previous Sunday, 17 September, and earlier in August, I had written a series of articles in the Irish edition of the *People* revealing a sinister new twist to a murder that had been committed thirteen years earlier. We reported, rightly, that a senior intelligence officer in the British Army had ordered the murder of a Belfast pensioner. The officer, who is still a serving captain in the Army, had set up the killing of sixty-seven-year-old Francisco Notorantonio at his west Belfast home in Ballymurphy, in October 1987. We further revealed that the FRU, the shadowy undercover squad that handled loyalist and republican agents, had ordered his murder in order to protect an IRA mole. The name of this mole would, in time, become synonymous with collusion and double-dealing: Stakeknife. We could get no further details at that time and there was scepticism within republican ranks about the existence of 'Steak Knife', or 'Stakeknife', as he was variously known. The name would soon be familiar to everyone.

We had quoted a Stevens Inquiry source as saying: 'There were no rules in this dirty war. Mr Notorantonio was sacrificed to protect Britain's most secret agent inside the IRA. It is now a question of who will win this struggle – Stevens or the Army. If Stevens wins and Steak Knife is exposed, it will be a disaster for the British government.'

The Ministry of Defence was not a bit pleased with the revelations. We had come close to identifying not only the agent, Stakeknife, but also one of Brian Nelson's handlers. The MOD's response was severe in the extreme – the desperate act of a department trying to keep its war secrets firmly in the classified cupboard. Britain's Defence Secretary, Geoff Hoon, authorised the spending of more than stg£100,000 of taxpayers' money on gagging the *People* newspaper. Neil Wallis was not to be found wanting. He poured tens of thousands of pounds into court cases as we pursued Hoon and his insupportable edicts. It took about a month before we succeeded in having most of the terms of the injunction lifted, albeit with a coda that insisted that any proposed attempt to identify or investigate agents or handlers had to be submitted, in writing, to the MOD three days prior to publication for approval. Needless to say, the *People* has never concurred with any of these conditions.

At the centre of all the allegations and counter-allegations, of course, was a family who had never got over the murder of a husband, father and grandfather. Francisco Notorantonio's daughter, Charlotte, told the *Sunday People* in 2000: 'We've wondered for thirteen years about the murder of my father. We are seeking a meeting with the Stevens's detectives. We want to know why our father was killed and we want those responsible brought to justice – not just the gunmen, but those in the Army who planned and ordered it.' I had interviewed the family about the allegations and it was difficult to explain to them the substitution of their father as a target in place of Stakeknife. They believed what I told them, however, and pursued the lead with vigour. Charlotte said: 'We always knew there was something not right about my father's murder. It didn't add up. We couldn't understand why they would target a man of his age who was in poor health, but it makes more sense now.'

Charlotte Notorantonio, like many families, is demanding an inquiry into her father's murder. It has been suggested to me, however, that the FRU destroyed all references to that murder after the *People* story of August 2000. That should come as no surprise.

At that time and ever since, many republicans who opposed the Good Friday Agreement used Stakeknife as a stick with which to beat Gerry Adams, blaming him for the undetected presence of an agent who had allegedly sacrificed active volunteers. There were suggestions on one website that Adams himself was the secret agent, with Tom Hartley, Alex Maskey, Martin McGuinness and others all suggested as possible informers. As a supporter of the Good Friday Agreement I found this very frustrating. Stakeknife was not involved in any way with the political side of republicanism and could not, as conspiracy theorists had suggested, have been involved in the long slow 'plot' to the political deal obtained by Sinn Féin.

Such fanciful theories also seriously hampered whistleblowers, such as Ingram, who were unwilling to identify agents but were frustrated that republicanism was beginning to fracture under the weight of the Stakeknife allegations, with reports of more and more IRA members joining dissident ranks as they became disillusioned with a peace process they saw as corrupt because of the presence at the negotiating table, as they believed, of an informer. It would have helped the peace process had Scappaticci been identified sooner as Stakeknife, and thereby taken out of the political equation entirely. As it was, it would be another three and a half years before the true identity of Stakeknife was heard in the public domain – an event the Ministry of Defence seemed to accept was inevitable, even if their agent did not. And even when Stakeknife was finally outed, in May 2003, it did not stop dissident republican conspiracy theorists from expending energy on the case, questioning the Notorantonio/Scappaticci/Nelson links at every turn. There were questions raised – some by Scappaticci himself, as part of his bluff, in a *Sunday Business Post* interview in August 2003 – over who knew what and when. The republican movement was in disarray, everyone blaming and suspecting everyone else.

Back in 2000, with my articles threatening to unmask Stakeknife, the Ministry of Defence was making sure that no one in the media could get close. Ingram's house was burgled in early 2000 and documents stolen – documents which were later produced in a court case held *in camera* where he was accused by the Ministry of Defence of giving information to newspapers in contravention of the Official Secrets Act. The *Sunday Times* was slapped with an injunction in early 2001 and its Northern Ireland Editor, Liam Clarke, threatened with being charged under the Official Secrets Act.

Ingram saw the files on the Notorantonio killing when working for the FRU. They were in the Stakeknife files. Ingram says: 'I read files which showed the loyalists were targeting Stakeknife and I discussed it with Stakeknife's handler. He confirmed loyalists had picked Scappaticci, among others. I also discussed it with Nelson's handler, who said basically that it had been taken care of. [Nelson's handler] told me: "A substitute has been put in place. It caused an almighty flap, but everything is back on track." This conversation was before the Notorantonio murder, and I had no idea how things were put "back on track". I learned after the killing that Notorantonio had been the substitute. My superiors and the handlers involved knew I was appalled by what had happened, that a pensioner had been killed. I was told to "shut up" and things got heated. I remember one of my senior officers said something like, "Didn't Gerry Adams carry the coffin? It couldn't have gone better for us." Another said, "We must take the war to the enemy. The end justifies the means." I thought it was wrong then and I still believe it is wrong. It was State-sponsored murder and the family of Mr Notorantonio deserves to know the truth.'

Senior officers would routinely write an end-of-year report for each FRU handler. At the end of 1990, Ingram's superior wrote in his confidential report: 'XXXXXX [Martin Ingram] must temper his comments when briefing senior Army officers.' The report was a recommendation for promotion, but the comment was clearly a reference to Ingram's numerous conversations with senior officers when he had questioned the FRU's role in a number of incidents. Ingram later recounted these heated exchanges to a senior investigating officer with the Stevens Inquiry, recalling in particular the murder of Notorantonio. That conversation was taped.

In the midst of this furore of collusion allegations, I received new allegations that further supported the claim that the security forces were involved, at some level, in collusion with paramilitary groups. These involved John McMichael – the UDA leader who ran a ruthless UFF campaign on the one hand and a new political strategy for the UDA aimed at ending the war on the other – and the claim that he had been allowed to die by the security forces, even though FRU handlers had been given at least ten warnings, which they passed to the RUC, that the IRA were going to kill him. McMichael, thirty-nine, was killed when a booby-trap bomb exploded under his car, which was parked outside his home in Hilden Court, Lisburn, in County Antrim on 22 December 1987. The IRA claimed responsibility. I was told by a new contact that McMichael had been the subject of ten death alerts. The source would not say where this information came from – whether the IRA or the UDA. He would only say that McMichael was allowed to die and that the security forces could have prevented the murder. However, senior RUC sources now say that they did receive warnings from Army intelligence, as well as from their own sources, and that McMichael was duly warned of an imminent IRA attack a fortnight before his murder. These sources say that McMichael stayed away from his home in the run-up to Christmas that year because of the warning he had received, which had been passed on to him by uniformed RUC officers. The new contact met me, briefly, near Gatwick Airport, London, after the allegations emerged. He stood by his claim, but refused to go any further, saying his life was in danger and he had decided he could not, or would not, say anymore. The meeting lasted less than five minutes.

Meanwhile, in early December 2000 Commander Hugh Orde, the police officer in charge of the day-to-day running of the Stevens Inquiry, now Chief Constable of the PSNI, agreed to meet with representatives of the Notorantonio family and their solicitor, Barra McGrory. Orde, known for his frankness, confirmed the existence of an agent called

Stakeknife, but not his identity, although his identity would have been known to Orde at that stage. Notorantonio's daughter, Charlotte, said afterwards: 'We were asking the Stevens team to investigate my father's murder. I asked if Stakeknife existed and they confirmed that he does exist. My father took a bullet for him so I told them it was vital they asked the Army for Stakeknife's files. We believe that Special Branch files on Tommy Lyttle are also vital to this investigation.' Indeed they were – and still are. Yet as far as we know Tommy Lyttle's Special Branch files have never been requested by the Stevens Inquiry. We believe it is imperative that they are handed over and examined, though in early September 2003 a contact of mine alleged that Lyttle's records had been destroyed by RUC Special Branch. The truth or falsehood of that allegation remains to be seen.

Orde's confirmation of Stakeknife's existence caused deep concern within the Provisional IRA. What little information the *Sunday Times* and the *People* had revealed about this agent led many to believe that Stakeknife, whoever he was, was still at the heart of the PIRA. The PIRA launched an inquiry into the allegations, but didn't get very far. In the 1980s, Freddie Scappaticci had briefly come under the scrutiny as a possible candidate for the real identity of Stakeknife, but he had weathered the storm and no one now believed that to be true. However, many in the republican movement believed Scappaticci was an informer for the security forces, even if he had denied it, although some republican sources insisted that Scappaticci had ceased his activities inside the IRA in January or February 1996. Whatever they did or did not believe about Scappaticci and his activities, the IRA had no idea that Scappaticci was the key FRU agent, Stakeknife.

The only people who had ever mentioned the name of Freddie Scappaticci in the early days were Lyttle and Nelson, and they had mentioned him only as a loyalist target. Lyttle died in 1995, before the existence of Stakeknife was uncovered, while Nelson died a month before Stakeknife's identity was exposed. We believe Nelson would have known Stakeknife's identity once the link between the Notorantonio murder and Scappaticci was made in the *People* in August and September of 2000, presuming, that is, that he saw the Irish editions of the paper, or had them sent over to his home in Cardiff.

The confirmation of the existence of a high-placed British Army agent within the ranks of the PIRA was perhaps the biggest fall-out from the murder of Francisco Notorantonio, and the effects of that fall-out are still being felt to this day. It started a cat-and-mouse game between the IRA, Sinn Féin, the media, the British Army and the British Government, each side blaming the other, each side seeking to limit the damage to itself. The story of Stakeknife, like the story of Brian Nelson, is one that the major players in Northern Ireland never wanted you to hear.

Chapter 13

Double Standards:
The Use and Abuse of Agents

Ingram/Harkin

The murky world of agents and informers gets even murkier when the interests of one agent overlap with those of another in a life-or-death situation. Which agent is more valuable? Is that ultimately what counts? The FRU and RUC Special Branch were sometimes in conflict about which agent to remove from action, when to protect an agent and how to deal with a conflict of interests. Here are two cases where Special Branch did not act in time. Our sources are detailed conversations within the FRU and Harkin's discussions with both police and republican sources.

Brendan 'Ruby' Davison

One of the most memorable images to be flashed around the world after Scappaticci was outed as the agent codenamed Stakeknife was a photograph of Gerry Adams carrying the coffin of murdered IRA man Brendan 'Ruby' Davison, with Scappaticci looking on in the background. It is impossible to know what the agent was thinking at the moment the shutter on the photographer's lense captured the image. Scappaticci was very close to Davison. In fact they were related through marriage and drank and socialised together. One local republican said of their friendship: 'They were inseparable, always looking our for each other. If there were rows in the Markets or Lower Ormeau they'd be together. I wouldn't be surprised if they both knew each other were Brussels sprouts [touts].' Scappaticci did knowthat Davison had been an informer. He had tried in vain to save Davison's life. That was the world inhabited by Scappaticci. One moment he would be helping to save a life; the next he'd be right in the middle of organising an informer's execution.

The deaths of Brendan Davison and Joe Fenton were just nine months apart. Both worked for RUC Special Branch. The two men were known to each other through the IRA but their deaths could not have been more different – Scappaticci was instrumental in the death of Fenton but had tried, through his handlers, to get Davison to safety before the IRA struck. In the end Davison was gunned down by a UVF gang that was undoubtedly given assistance from within the RUC, and there is some evidence in this respect.

Brendan Davison was, like many teenagers in the early 1970s, caught up in the Troubles of the times. He joined the Fianna, the IRA's junior wing, in 1971 when he was just sixteen and progressed into the IRA itself less than a year later. A meat porter by trade, he was from Joy Street in the Markets area of Belfast and was said to be well-liked by friends and neighbours. In February 1974, aged just eighteen, he was convicted of the attempted murder on St Patrick's Day the previous year of a British soldier, and sentenced to fifteen years.

Davison claimed that he was forced to make a confession, that every time he denied involvement in the incident an intelligence officer poked him in the stomach. Later, he claimed, the officer held his hand over a jar of acid and threatened to burn him if he didn't own up. Davison told the court: 'I said that I had done it, but I didn't. I was terrified. I made the statement to the police because I thought if I had not I would be sent back to the Army for more treatment.' When the fifteen-year sentence was handed down, Davison's mother shouted from the public gallery, 'My son is innocent.'

Republican sources still insist Davison was innocent of the charges against him in the case, but admit he had been involved in the shooting of Army defector Ranger Louis Hammond. Innocent or guilty, Brendan Davison went to Long Kesh and came out more hardened than ever before. His release came just before the 1981 hunger strikes. Northern Ireland had been plunged into a new spiral of violence and it wasn't long before Davison was back in custody, this time on the evidence of a supergrass. He spent a year – December 1982 to December 1983 – behind bars, on the word of John Morgan.

We are not privy to the circumstances of his recruitment as an agent by the RUC. Perhaps he feared the possibility or even the threat of another prison sentence – Davison was now twenty-eight, and had spent his best years behind bars. Once he was onside, money and good handling would keep him on board. The IRA tended to trust ex-prisoners more than most, and the longer such people had served the better their credibility. He rose to the rank of OC of the IRA in the Markets area of Belfast. Special Branch had recruited a valuable informer, but one whom they ultimately sacrificed when he was no longer of any use to them.

Davison was shot four times and wounded in a UVF gun

attack at a bookie's shop in Belfast on 30 May 1987 and lost the use of one of his arms as a result. He was ordered to rest and recuperate but he wanted to maintain his role as OC. He came under suspicion from fellow IRA members after a number of arrests and arms finds in the latter part of 1987. Freddie Scappaticci was briefed by Northern Command that there was a question mark over Davison and that he would have to take Davison in for questioning. Scappaticci informed his FRU handlers that, at some stage, he was going to have to pull Ruby Davison in for a grilling by the Nutting Squad. Numerous MISR reports were generated detailing Scappaticci's warnings. Ingram knows that every single one of those warnings was passed to RUC Special Branch.

However, before the Nutting Squad got to Davison, at 9.05am on 25 July 1988, an armed UVF member, equipped with a map locating Davison's home and a picture of Davison – supplied by Brian Nelson – called into a taxi office on the Castlereagh Road in the east of the city and asked a driver to take him to Dundonald. Once inside the taxi, he put on a mask and ordered the driver to take him instead to Ballarat Street on the Ravenhill Road. The driver was then ordered out of the orange Vauxhall Cavalier and another armed and masked man got in. The two drove to another street where they met up with a third UVF man. All three now changed into stolen RUC uniforms. Shortly after 9.30am the gang pulled up outside Davison's home, in Friendly Way in the Markets area. Two of them got out of the car. One knocked on the front door and shouted: 'It's the police, open up.' Davison did so, as he had done an hour earlier when real police officers had visited his house to deliver a summons. The other UVF man at the door opened fire, shooting nine times into the hallway. A local man chased the getaway car in his own vehicle. He recalls: 'I saw three men drive off in an orange-coloured Vauxhall Cavalier over the Albert Bridge. There was a guy in the back with blonde hair taking off a green jacket. He was laughing. The car drove on towards the Albertbridge Road and I lost them.'

In the days that followed, the IRA decided not to divulge its belief that Davison was a Special Branch informer. In fact he was given an IRA funeral and a volley of shots was fired near a mural in Ardoyne. Five days after the murder *An Phoblacht*, the republican newspaper, carried a front-page tribute which read 'to his comrades he was a solid and trustworthy volunteer of immense experience and courage'. The same edition carried a small apology to the relatives of a family wiped out in an IRA 'mistake' on the border just two days before Davison's death: Robert Hanna, 45, his wife Maureen, 44, and their seven-year-old son David had died in a land-mine explosion at Killeen, outside Newry. They were return-ing home from a holiday in the United States when an IRA bomb team mistook their car for one being driven along the same route by High Court Judge Eoin Higgins. It had been another dark disgusting week in Northern Ireland.

Scappaticci's handler has confirmed to Ingram that Davi-son was a Branch agent, and a very successful one, although initially the republican movement would not acknowledge in public the speculation which had been rife since his assas-sination. In private, though, the movement must have known that Davison was indeed a well placed and damaging agent. How did they know? Scap had been investigating Davison for a few months previous to his murder and his information led to numerous MISR reports. Scap's handler also confirmed Stakeknife's involvement in the internal security unit's investigation, and that Brian Nelson was heavily involved in the targeting of Davison and that a number of reports were sent to the RUC who appeared 'not very interested'. Ingram saw an RUC report detailing that the uniforms used in the attack were stolen from Mountpottinger police station. Ironically, Davison's Branch handlers were also stationed there. RUC source reports give a very graphic account of Davison's murder, indicating that they either had an agent *on* the murder team or at least had very good access to the operational details. Scap's handler himself was baffled as to why the RUC allowed their agent to be murdered.

Davison's death raises serious questions about the rule of law in Northern Ireland. Regardless of whether Davison was an IRA member or a Special Branch informant, he should have been warned by the Branch that his life was in danger. He was facing death from two fronts – his own side and loyalists. Even from the point of view of their own credibility, Special Branch could and should have moved in to save him – that they didn't would make any future would-be informants think long and hard before passing information to the Branch.

The question also has to be asked whether FRU handlers actually *helped* Brian Nelson target Davison. They did provide intelligence, which UDA man Nelson happily gave to the UVF who carried out the murder. As a FRU operative, Ingram understood that FRU officers believed Davison would never actually be a target for assassination a second time. They believed the Branch would pull their agent out of harm's way. But they didn't.

Joseph Fenton

Joseph Fenton, an estate agent in west Belfast, began working for the RUC Special Branch in 1982. He was, from that year until his death in 1989, their best agent inside the IRA. Fenton supplied the IRA with vacant houses for holding meetings and storing weapons and explosives, so that throughout that period the police were able to bug meetings of the Army Council, Northern Command and Belfast Brigade staff. Republican sources believe that Fenton's work led to the compromising of dozens of IRA operations, including the March 1988 'Death on the Rock' killings in which the SAS shot dead three unarmed IRA members in Gibraltar after plans were discussed in one of the houses he made available. Police were also able to disarm explosive devices and 'jark', or bug, IRA weapons. A former Special Branch officer familiar with some of Fenton's work said: 'Joe devastated the IRA in west Belfast in the mid-1980s. I was told he loved his work and got a great deal of pleasure after operations were compromised. He was a very willing agent and tried on at least two occasions to entrap senior republicans. But it was probably only a matter of time before he was caught out and by late 1988 he was under suspicion.'

Freddie Scappaticci, in reports to his handlers, warned that Fenton was indeed suspected of helping the security forces after a tracking device was found inside a weapon stored in one of his vacant properties. The internal security unit warned the IRA to stop using these properties. Special Branch decided to pull Fenton out of Northern Ireland. They moved him to England, but Fenton – like Scappaticci some years later – believed he could bluff it out. He asked Andrew Hunter, a

Conservative MP, for help. Hunter contacted police, who were absolutely clear about what would happen if Joe Fenton returned to Northern Ireland. Hunter, now a member of the DUP, said later: 'Special Branch told me that if he came home he would be killed very quickly. They warned me he was a marked man and that it was dangerous to be associated with him and I passed this on to him, but he still went back.'

Not only did Fenton go back, but he continued to pass information to police. In early February 1989 a planned IRA mortar bomb attack was thwarted and six IRA volunteers arrested after a massive police operation in west Belfast. It was to be Joe Fenton's last operation for Special Branch.

On 24 February 1989, the IRA abducted Fenton and took him to a house at Carrigart Avenue, in the Lenadoon area of west Belfast. The householder, James Martin, was convicted of the false imprisonment of Fenton during the Danny Morrison trial (*see* Chapter 7). Martin described his role in the Fenton murder to police during an interrogation at Castlereagh police station on 11 January 1990, three days after his arrest, along with Morrison, for the false imprisonment of informer Sandy Lynch. He described the events surrounding the death of Joe Fenton as follows:

'I want to tell you about another incident which happened last year [Fenton]; it is the same as happened last weekend [the Lynch case]. It started when I was working for Sinn Féin in the Westminster elections. I did some canvassing and on the day of the election I did sort of a transport manager for anyone who couldn't get down to vote. After the elections I wasn't really involved with

Sinn Féin, it is only at election time. After this in February last year a man, the same man that approached me this time, came to my house and asked me if it would be all right to use the house for interrogation. It was a Friday when this man came to my house; he said it would be used the following day. I said it would be all right and he went away.

'On the next day, a Saturday – it was after dark, I'm not sure of the time – two men came to my house. I opened the door to let them in. They said that I was expecting them so I brought them into the house, they went into the sitting room and sat down. These two men are two out of the three who came to my house last Friday [the Lynch case]. One was sitting on the settee and one was sitting on the armchair.

'They were in the house for a couple of minutes and then there was a knock at the door. One of them got up to answer it, I'm not sure which one; he let some people in and the other fella went out to the hall. I heard people going up the stairs, I heard them going into the spare bedroom – I had told the two men they could use that room. When they got into the room there was a lot of thumping and banging like there was a fight going on, it carried on for about five minutes. After that there was the odd bit of thumping and the occasional raised voice. I knew someone was being interrogated but I hadn't seen him. I don't know how many people were involved upstairs but I think it was more than the first two men.

'After a while one of the men came down and asked for a cup of tea. I went into the kitchen and showed him where the things were, I didn't stay to see how many cups he made. This fella went back up the stairs with the tea. I'm not sure what time that this was. There was more shouting. I think that this fella they were interrogating was stronger than Lynch. I remember that night the Tyson and Bruno fight was on from Las Vegas, as one of the men from upstairs came down and watched a bit of the fight. He only watched part of it then went back upstairs. I turned off the TV before the fight ended and I went up to bed then. I went to bed and I could still hear the people in the back bedroom. I went to sleep after a while.

'I got up on the Sunday morning, about ten or maybe half nine. I went downstairs and made tea myself. One of the men came down and asked for tea. We made tea and a load of toast; it was put on one plate. He took it upstairs and things seemed to be a lot quieter than the night before but I could still hear that there was people upstairs. I'm not exactly sure, but I think one of them came down for food later in the day and he went back up with it.

'I knew that they were still in the upstairs room and later on in the afternoon, after it was dark, one of the men came down to me in the kitchen. He said to me that they would be leaving soon and he stood at the kitchen window. He must have unlocked the front door, for a girl walked in just after that. The girl came right into the kitchen. When she came in, I walked out of the kitchen into the sitting room. This girl was about five-foot-five tall and average build. She was in ordinary clothes, I don't remember just what she wore. I don't know where the girl went. I was in the sitting room and about five or ten minutes had gone by and I heard some noise out on the stairs. The fella from the kitchen opened the sitting-room door and stuck his head in. He said something like, "We are away now and somebody will call for what is left up there." I heard the door closing and the house was quiet. I knew they were all gone.

'About two minutes later I heard some cracks that I knew were shots. I stayed in the house for a few minutes, then I went outside. I heard some kids saying there was a man lying up near Oliver Plunkett [school]. When I first heard the shots I thought they had run into the Army, but when I thought about it I had an idea that they had shot the man. I went back home and went up into the back bedroom. There was two of our chairs in the room, and I took them downstairs. There was bandages and cotton wool and white tape in the back bedroom. I gathered it all together in plastic bags and took it downstairs for someone to collect. Nobody ever came for that stuff so I split it up around the house, so when they asked me for the bandages this time [the Lynch case] I had it in the house already.

'I remember it was on the TV that a man had been shot and the cameras showed round by Oliver Plunkett School and the body covered up. I heard later that this man's name was Joseph Fenton. This was the first time I knew that the men in the house were IRA. They were more careful the first time and I only ever saw two different men. The second time [the Lynch case] they trusted me more and they were open in their movements. I forgot to say that these men also left behind a pair of tan leather gloves. I put these away after the first interrogation, and I think they used them for the second.'

The thumping and banging James Martin had heard that Saturday and Sunday in February 1989 was Freddie Scappaticci torturing Fenton – one State agent interrogating another. Scappaticci had earlier informed his handlers of Fenton's whereabouts and that he, Scappaticci, would be carrying out the interrogation. His handlers had passed on these urgent reports to RUC Special Branch but the police did nothing. Perhaps there was nothing they could do, or perhaps they believed such a high-profile agent would face interrogation for a few more days and they were awaiting the arrival of an Army Council representative to pass sentence on Fenton. Perhaps the police were more concerned about not wanting to compromise Stakeknife.

Regardless, the British Army's top agent had a hand in the killing of the Branch's top agent. Scappaticci had now tried twice to save the life of Joe Fenton and when the authorities failed to act he protected himself, maintaining his role in the Nutting Squad and ensuring Fenton would die.

As always Scappaticci recorded his evidence, with Joe Fenton reading a statement into a tape recorder. The sound of a saucepan being banged can be heard before Fenton begins his confession. The taped confession lasts ten minutes. At James Martin's subsequent trial Joe Fenton's father, Patrick, said his son had told him how Special Branch had pressurised him into working for them. He also said that two days after his son's body was found he was played a tape recording at Sinn Féin offices of his son's final plea for mercy. Fenton had been shot three times through the head and once in the chest, in an alleyway in Bunbeg Park, beside Oliver Plunkett School. 'The last part of the tape was that Joseph asked for mercy to be given and be allowed to go home to his wife and kids, but this was not done. As you know, Joseph was shot,' Mr Fenton told Belfast Crown Court.

Also on the tape are details of how, seven years earlier, Fenton had sacrificed the lives of two other agents to protect himself. In this case, in September 1985, Scappaticci's Nutting Squad had pulled the trigger on Catherine and Gerard Mahon, a woman and her husband who were Special Branch agents. They too were allowed to die by the security forces. And the sickening twist is that another informer saved in the incident, Fenton, was also later sacrificed. The bloody murders of the Mahons shocked a country grown used to such killings, because a woman had been shot. The first ever killing of a female IRA informer was condemned on all sides.

It is claimed, by both republicans and security sources, that suspicion fell upon the couple when a number of IRA operations were compromised. Freddie Scappaticci and his Nutting Squad were called in to investigate. Fenton admitted in his confession that he had directed Scappaticci and the IRA towards the Mahons to deflect attention away from himself after a number of safe houses were compromised. There is no suggestion that either knew the other was an agent for the State at that stage. Both Gerard and Catherine Mahon confessed to working for the RUC. They had been receiving payments of between £20 and £200 for tip-offs about republican activity. Payments increased for weapons finds or arrests. The Mahons' flat in Twinbrook was fitted with elaborate bugging devices to monitor IRA active service units each time they used the premises.

Acting on Fenton's information, Scappaticci and three other members of his unit took the Mahons to Norglen

Crescent in Turf Lodge to be executed. What happened next is known only to the IRA security unit members who were present. According to some sources both Mahons confessed, but the IRA had planned to kill only Gerard Mahon. It is claimed Catherine Mahon was shot in the back as she tried to escape. Mahon, a mechanic, was twenty-eight, his wife just twenty-seven. A local man said at the time: 'We heard two bursts of gunfire and then a car was driven away at high speed. We went out and discovered the girl. We thought she was dead. We tried first aid but the side of her head was blown away. A young lad came up to us saying there was a man lying in the entry a bit further up and still alive. We got to him and he was badly wounded. He was struggling to breathe and choking on his own blood. He had been hit in the side of the head and the face. Whatever is behind it all, it's ridiculous. Those responsible are animals. Nothing justifies murder. They had both been tied by their wrists – but they must have broken free by struggling when they realised what was going to happen.' The SDLP's Dr Joe Hendron remarked: 'This slaughter has few equals in barbarity and it proves the Provo idea of justice is warped. It makes us all sick.'

But there was blood on many hands. Scappaticci informed his handlers of the IRA's suspicions about the Mahons and that information was passed to Special Branch. Nothing was done to save the Mahons. Once again an Army agent was involved in the abduction, torture, interrogation and murder of RUC agents.

Chapter 14

Face-to-Face with Scappaticci

Harkin

As I walked to the front door of Freddie Scappaticci's west Belfast home, I was surprised to see a smart silver BMW parked in the driveway – as far as everyone knew, Scappaticci was not at home. Republicans and security force sources alike were convinced that the man who was once at the heart of the IRA's security unit was safely out of harm's way, perhaps in an Army base in Britain. It was 8.10pm on Saturday, 10 May 2003, and Scappaticci had just been named on an American spy website as Stakeknife, the jewel in the crown of the British Army's network of agents inside the republican movement. To my surprise, after about two minutes my knock at the door of the house in Riverdale, in the heart of Andersonstown, was answered. The young boy who opened the door turned away to a rear living room and shouted, 'Granda, there's somebody at the door.' A short, stocky, muscular man appeared in the hallway, dressed in shorts, socks and a football T-shirt with the word 'Italia' on the breast above a small Italian tricolour.

'Freddie Scappaticci?' I asked, as the man came towards me. 'Yes,' he said. Before he could say any more I told him, 'Freddie, I'm Greg Harkin, and I'm –' Scappaticci interrupted me before I could say I was a journalist from the *People* newspaper. 'Come on in, Greg,' he said. I introduced John Rush, the photographer who accompanied me, and Scappaticci waved him into the hallway, before locking the vestibule door behind us and putting the key in his pocket. This worried me for two reasons – firstly, the locking of a door behind you can be frightening, especially when the man turning the key could be a multiple murderer; and secondly, Freddie Scappaticci knew exactly who I was. I had been writing about him for three years, albeit under his agent codename Stakeknife. But this was just the start of Scappaticci's bluff.

Scappaticci appeared calm and collected on the outside but I felt, and this is only a feeling, that under that cool exterior he was seething with anger as I showed him a copy of an article due to appear the next day, Sunday. I now know that Scappaticci was an avid reader of both the *People* and the *Sunday Times* because of coverage of Stakeknife in both papers and because Liam Clarke, the *Sunday Times* Northern Ireland Editor, had actually telephoned Scappaticci on a number of occasions. So Scappaticci knew very well that I was a journalist from the *People*. I didn't need to introduce myself. I now also know that he had been warned two days earlier by his handlers, who still valued his views on republicans, that he may well be named on websites and perhaps newspapers prior to the weekend. If Scappaticci was worried, he didn't show it as we walked into the living room.

I told him why I was there – I had had a tip-off an hour earlier that he had left his home, apparently with the help of a mass of British soldiers and police officers, complete with a furniture van. He shook his head, held the piece of paper with the story and began his denials.

'I'm not the same Freddie Scappaticci that all these claims are being made about,' he said. 'I haven't been involved in politics for the past thirteen years.' I asked him if he knew or was related to any other Freddie Scappaticcis or Alfredo Scappaticcis (I knew handlers sometimes called him Alfredo). He insisted: 'I'm not Alfredo, but yes, I do know some other Alfredos.' This, of course, was another lie. He continued: 'Listen, right, I'm not that person there [pointing to the article] and I'd be concerned that you'll mix me up with someone else. It's a real concern. People could put two and two together and get five. I just know it's not me referred to.'

I told him it had been alleged that Stakeknife had received up to £80,000 a year to infiltrate the IRA and take out top IRA members who had been wrongly branded as touts. Scappaticci, whose shorts were covered in dust, pointed downwards and protested: 'Listen, I've been building blocks all day. Does it look as if I've been getting £80,000 a year?' He went quiet for what was probably ten seconds, but the silence seemed to last an hour. I asked him again about his republican links. 'This must be someone else, because it's not me,' he said. 'It's ten years since I was involved with politics. Do you think I'd be here if it was me?' I said I didn't know, but I was interested to know what his involvement in politics was. He told me: 'I was in politics for a long time, but I'm not now, and that's really it.' He had dismissed his entire career as Britain's most notorious civil servant in just sixteen words.

Scappaticci continued trying to convince me that he wasn't the agent Stakeknife: 'I don't even know what this person Stakeknife was supposed to have been. I've never heard of it. What is he supposed to have done?' I explained again that Stakeknife was a British agent inside the

Provisional IRA, and that it was being alleged he was that agent. 'Who's saying this, because they've got it wrong,' he insisted. 'I know a few other Freddie Scappaticcis, and there's probably more that I don't know, so there must be a mix-up somewhere. I'm Fred, but I'm not Alfredo or Freddie. It says there that I'm getting this money. Would I be living here with this sort of money if I had it?' I asked him if he had relatives of the same name and he replied, 'No, not that I know of.'

John Rush nodded to me and I knew it was time to go. I said that I'd be in touch, wrote a telephone number down on a piece of notepaper and handed it to him. 'Give me a call if you want to talk any more,' I said. 'I'll see,' he replied. He took a key from his pocket and opened the vestibule door and we left.

As we left the house, my instinct told me that I had just met Stakeknife, but this was tempered by nagging doubts brought on by his claim that there were other Freddie Scappaticcis. I had arrived at Scappaticci's house poorly prepared, as I hadn't expected him to be there.

I had tried many times over the previous two years to obtain a picture of Scappaticci, but it was too dangerous, both for Scappaticci and myself. Every photographer in Belfast knew I had been writing about Stakeknife and any request for a picture of Scappaticci might have alerted them to his identity. I had spent hours trawling through newspapers, hoping to catch a glimpse of Scappaticci, but to no avail. It was like looking for a needle in a haystack, especially as I couldn't check him out with any republican contacts.

Things had now changed substantially. I drove to a republican contact's home in west Belfast. The area is like a village in many ways, and the outing of Scappaticci was already being discussed widely. The first contact I spoke to hadn't seen Scappaticci since 1995, and wasn't even sure if he was still in Northern Ireland. Another said it was 1989 since he had seen him and believed he had moved to Dublin in mid-1996. Another reporter had been busy chasing Scappaticci south of the border. But the woman who answered the phone at his former residence was suspicious, and said that she had no idea where Scappaticci was now. We contacted his address in west Dublin, but the woman I spoke to refused to confirm whether Scappaticci was still in the Dublin area or in Northern Ireland. 'I can't say where he is at the minute,' she said. 'He was here some time ago, but is not now. I can't say for sure where he is at the minute. But if you tell me who's calling, I can get a message to him for you.'

We had to get our own photograph. By 9.30 we were back at Scappaticci's house. This time he came to the door himself. I told him, 'Listen, if you are Stakeknife my advice would be to get out, and get out as soon as possible. If you are not Stakeknife my advice would be to take precautions, because as far as everyone is concerned you are Stakeknife.' He replied, 'I am concerned that anyone would say we had left our home in this area. My wife is away all right – she's on a pilgrimage to Fatima. It's a different Freddie Scappaticci you are looking for.' As we talked, John Rush took a picture from his car.

At 10pm I called three different security sources and each confirmed that I had just met Stakeknife. As far as they were concerned the big secret was out, Stakeknife's identity was in the public domain. But another contact insisted that Stakeknife was 'safe', that he was out of the country already. Later that night we showed the digital image of Scappaticci to three different republican contacts. Each of them confirmed that he was the same Freddie Scappaticci, or 'Scap', who had worked for the IRA's internal security unit.

Later that evening I would be prevented from telling the whole story of what Scappaticci said by lawyers worried that I might be in breach of part of a Ministry of Defence injunction. This was also just before Martin Ingram was due to give evidence to the Saville Inquiry, where he was prevented from discussing security force files by a Public Interest Certificate issued by Britain's Ministry of Defence. There were new fears of a major censorship clampdown.

However, we went with the story on page one, complete with Scappaticci's denials from my interview with him. The Irish *Sunday Tribune* and the *Sunday Herald*, based in Glasgow, had also gone with the story, albeit placing Stakeknife in protective military custody.

Scappaticci's denials didn't add up – there were no other Freddie Scappaticcis or Alfredo Scappaticcis who had been on the IRA's Northern Command. It was also strange that he had invited me into his home without even a question. By now I had no doubts. A Ministry of Defence official told me that even he had been misled, that he had been assured by colleagues that Stakeknife was out of Northern Ireland. He now accepted that Scappaticci was at home.

Later that Sunday afternoon Scappaticci met his handlers, near Portaferry on County Down's Ards Peninsula. He was taken to a safe house to be debriefed. He had been warned weeks earlier, and again the previous Wednesday, Thursday, Friday and Saturday, that his name could leak out. But Scappaticci decided he would stay put; he would brass it out, deny he was an informer.

defamation proceedings. The past three days have been very traumatic for Mr Scappaticci who now intends to resume his private life.'

Reporters Rowan and Cadwallader would not be given the opportunity to question either the statement or Scappaticci's role. Rowan tried, asking why Scappaticci thought he had been linked to Stakeknife. Scappaticci replied, 'I don't know.' Questioned about whether he had ever been involved in the IRA or the republican movement, Scappaticci hesitated before replying, 'I was involved in the republican movement thirteen years ago, but I have had no involvement in this past thirteen years.' Mr Flanigan then ended the interview and Scappaticci scurried back through the door from which he had emerged just minutes earlier.

Sinn Féin appeared to accept his statement. Gerry Kelly, the party's policing spokesman, said the Scappaticci family were victims of 'nameless, faceless people' and called on the government to explain what was going on. 'The files must be opened up and there must be full disclosure,' he said. The same theme was repeated by republicans over subsequent weeks – that Scappaticci was not an informer. Yet to seasoned observers, the fact that he had not appeared alongside Sinn Féin leaders at a press conference left a question mark over his role. Some republican sources were willing to admit, off the record of course, that there had been a question mark over Scappaticci both in 1990 in the Sandy Lynch case and again in late 1995. On both occasions Scappaticci had denied working for the security forces but, nevertheless, he was stood down in early 1996.

The Stakeknife debate soon switched to the two parliaments – the Commons in London and Dáil Éireann in Dublin.

Taoiseach Bertie Ahern, in a statement which stunned TDs, told the Dáil that when he raised intelligence matters with the British he was usually less wise afterwards than before. The British came under pressure from Labour MP Kevin McNamara to open an investigation into the activities of the agent Stakeknife. The former shadow Northern Ireland spokesman said Scappaticci should be questioned by the Stevens Inquiry. He said of Scappaticci: 'He would be guilty of colluding in the murders of IRA volunteers, police officers, soldiers and civilians ... If true, these allegations go to the heart of British involvement in unlawful actions in pursuit of its objectives in Northern Ireland ... I believe the public has been kept in the dark for too long. I believe the [British] government has colluded in unlawful activities of its agents. I believe those that are guilty must be called to account – however high up.' Conservative and unionist members, however, said that intelligence matters should remain secret to protect sources. Conservative MP Patrick Mercer said he had encountered many horrors as a platoon commander in Northern Ireland in the early 1970s, but 'it was made clear we acted at all times within the law because acting outside the law made us criminals and made us terrorists in our own right.' He added that he hoped no prosecution would take place.

Scappaticci's bluff was paying off. He was back living in west Belfast and appeared on the front page of the *Andersonstown News*, a local weekly paper, repeating his denials, albeit confining his entire history in the internal security unit to one sentence. The same paper would later accept, many months later, that most people had reached their 'own sad conclusions' that Scappaticci was an informer.

There was another development a week later when Liam Clarke, the *Sunday Times* journalist who first disclosed the existence of an agent called Stakeknife whilst a reporter at the *Sunday News*, revealed a new twist. Clarke reported that Danny Morrison's suspicion of entrapment in the Sandy Lynch case was being investigated by Stevens as part of his probe into the activities of Scappaticci. The case, Clarke wrote, was passed to Stevens by Nuala O'Loan, the Northern Ireland Police ombudsman, in January 2003. Clarke revealed: '[O'Loan] found no evidence of police misconduct but was concerned that Stakeknife had been involved in the interrogation of Lynch. O'Loan discovered that the judge, the defence and the investigating detectives in Morrison's trial were not told of Stakeknife's role. Had they known, the information may have added weight to Morrison's defence. Morrison had claimed he was present to take Lynch to a press conference with an allegation that [Lynch's] RUC handlers had put pressure on him to set up two prominent republicans. It was suggested in court that he had been there to pass sentence of death on behalf of the IRA Army Council. Morrison said: "We want the conviction overturned and my solicitor Barra McGrory has made the first move by approaching Nuala O'Loan. I want to know if she received information that would allow us to go to the court of criminal appeal." He claimed that Lynch had reached a deal with the IRA whereby he would publicly name his police handlers and accuse them of urging him to set up a "shoot-to-kill operation" against IRA suspects. Morrison said: "I want to know if any agent set me up. I believe that the ombudsman was told that it was the agent codenamed Stakeknife who was involved in my case. I want to know if I was entrapped."'

O'Loan's investigators had met myself and Ingram the previous August to discuss Stakeknife. Our understanding at the time of writing is that the case has been passed to Sir John Stevens for investigation. Only after that investigation will O'Loan's office decide whether it requires further investigation or a review. Scappaticci launched his own legal action in late May, seeking to force the British government to 'clear his name' as he put it. He claimed that his life had been placed in danger by the allegations, which he had publicly denied, and sought a judicial review to make the Northern Ireland security minister, Jane Kennedy, confirm that he had not been a British agent.

At the beginning of June, Scappaticci had very different worries – convincing the IRA leadership that he wasn't an informer, that he wasn't the agent everyone else believed him to be. He was summoned to the village of Creeslough in County Donegal to be questioned. The PSNI tipped off Gardaí, who kept a close watch on his movements as well as his conversations with the two senior IRA officers. Both of these men are originally from Northern Ireland, but have been living in County Donegal for more than a decade. Both are experienced interrogators and have interviewed members during internal inquires on a number of previous occasions. They are both businessmen, who we are not allowed to name for legal reasons.

Scappaticci lost his legal action on August 18, 2003. Meanwhile Jane Kennedy consistently refused to make any statement, saying that the government did not comment on intelligence matters, including the naming of agents. Scappaticci's lawyers invoked the European convention on human rights and he was given leave for the review in the high court in Belfast. But finally the lord chief justice, Lord Carswell, dismissed his application to have Ms Kennedy's decision overturned. He said that to deny one person as an agent could place the life of another in danger. It was clear the British were never going to introduce a new policy of identifying informers. Scappaticci, recently returned from a month-long holiday in Italy, was not in court.

By this time republicans were briefing journalists that they now accepted Scappaticci was an agent. But at the end of the month Scappaticci decided to do another interview, this time with the *Sunday Business Post*. Again his entire career inside the IRA was reduced to a single paragraph. There were no probing questions and no forthcoming answers. Indeed the allegations about the 'Cook Report' tapes were not, it seems, even put to Scappaticci. The interview was simply a repeat of his bluff and his claim that the 'false allegations' had ruined his life. Reporter Barry O'Kelly quoted Scappaticci as saying: 'I'm a lifelong republican and my reputation's destroyed. I'm just taking one day at a time. I couldn't tell you what I'll be doing in six months. I don't know what the future will hold, I'm only fifty-seven, I've another eight years before retirement. I'm just a working class man and now I can't go out to work. My life's been turned upside down. I'm not a religious person, but I've been in touch with the priests. It's for spiritual help ... I'm talking now because stories keep appearing every week in the newspapers up here. I want to continue with my action against the British government, because at the end of the day they are responsible for the security services, the people who are behind all this. But in the meantime the stories are getting more fantastic by the week.'

Scappaticci was said to be suffering from depression. But he had done so long before he was named as Stakeknife. Liam Clarke, who has followed the affair for fifteen years, reported: 'Occasionally I rang Scappaticci, and he didn't seem to fit the stereotype of an IRA hardman. He arranged to meet me once, but pulled out citing ill health. I learned he was being treated for depression and was thinking of moving to southern Italy where his family originated.'

There was also speculation that Scappaticci was a double agent, that this was why the IRA had not moved against him. Ingram says: 'He was not a double agent. He was an agent who killed his own people. Simple as that.' Anthony McIntyre, a former IRA commander turned academic, wrote an internet article speculating that 'the IRA already knew his identity, debriefed him some time ago and have remained silent since – a bit like the British did in the case of Anthony Blunt.' Ingram agrees. But he insists today: 'I can see how the allegations became uncomfortable for republicans, but there was a silver lining on that cloud; it meant dissidents could no longer argue that Stake was a political figure behind the entire peace process. As far as republicans are concerned Stakeknife can do no more damage. It's over. I believe the damage is to the British government in that one of their agents was involved in murder, often in the murder of other agents. It was wrong.'

Chapter 15

Fallout for a Whistleblower

Ingram

Over the last twenty years there have been many allegations made against the security and intelligence agencies in Northern Ireland, for example, the 'shoot-to-kill' allegations, allegations of collusion, etc. The majority of these allegations have, of course, been made by those who waged war upon the security forces. What is surprising is how few people within the security agencies have raised concerns, either contemporaneously, or later. The reason I find this surprising is because the vast majority of members of the Intelligence Corps that I served with were decent people with solid moral values. I am disappointed that more of my fellow soldiers have not come forward to add to the debate – even those who come forward to defend illegal actions should be encouraged, if for no other reason than to inform and educate the public. For many people it has been difficult reconciling the truth with the deliberate misinformation which has been placed in the public domain. Of course that is a legitimate tactic, an essential part of any war, and has been employed over the years by the Ministry of Defence and the RUC with great success.

Unfortunately much of this chaff has been swallowed by the written press and, whether by design or not, they have contributed in creating the haze that has made it difficult for members of the public to see the wood for the trees. It is true that there are those in the press who enjoy a cosy relationship with elements of the establishment, whether that be the Police, the Army or those within the political sphere. These journalists are fed titbits or stories, which portray a certain perspective and can amount to little more than propaganda. This arrangement is not and cannot be good for a genuinely informed society, or indeed for a believable press. There are also those in the press who have sat on stories at the request of police officers, not because there was no truth in the story, but because the truth was unpalatable. I know of one incident where a very, very senior police officer even spoke to a journalist's editor to pull a story. This senior policeman told lies and it was only after the truth was demonstrated that the story, which involved a contentious murder, could be told for the first time. That police officer was later to apologise with a wry smile.

The recent unmasking of Stakeknife has caused confusion and apprehension among grass-roots republicans as well as within the British security establishment. Although the agent was an Army asset, he was well known to both the RUC and the security service (MI5), both of whom benefited from his information and participated in setting up his tasks.

During the late part of 1999 the MOD sought and received an injunction against both Martin Ingram (but under his own name) and the *Sunday Times* newspaper who first published an honest and accurate account of that individual's experiences whilst serving within both the Intelligence Corps and the FRU. During these proceedings, an affidavit was sworn in relation to the 'Frank Hegarty' incident, which explained to the judge that the former member of the FRU was a danger to national security because he had knowledge which was potentially damaging to 'national security'. The affidavit was immoral in my opinion, because its intention was to make sure this former soldier and whistleblower did not explain to the public the role that FRU agent Stakeknife played in the murder of his fellow informer Frank Hegarty.

There has been recent press speculation suggesting that Sir John Stevens, the London Metropolitan Police Commissioner, was about to seek to interview Stakeknife in connection with a number of murders. Any interview would be in connection with Sir John's inquiries into 'collusion' between security forces and illegal paramilitaries. I for one would be very surprised if Stakeknife was interviewed. Why? Well, over three years ago I discussed the involvement of Stakeknife with Hugh Orde and his team of investigators. It was clear to me then that they were already well aware of his identity.

To be clear, if Sir John wanted, he could have made a move years ago, and carried out a thorough investigation into the activities of both Stakeknife and, more importantly, the methods of operating employed by the security and intelligence agencies. If, and it is a big 'if', Sir John publicly enters the Stakeknife arena, in my opinion he will have done so reluctantly and with one eye on the clock as he is close to retirement. Such an inquiry would make the Brian Nelson affair look like a tame 'Jackanory' story.

A by-product of the unmasking of Stakeknife has been the comfort that those who view republicans as the enemy have enjoyed. They have rejoiced in the temporary disruption that the republican movement is suffering. Personally I hope they choke on their laughter, because this subject transcends personal grievances. For those who have gloated within the security forces, I should point out that the disruption is temporary. When the smoke clears from the battlefield, we will be no further forward. To gloat after so much death and destruction and not learn the lessons is disgusting.

I would suggest that if you were in the republican movement you would be appalled that a senior 'hands-on' player could operate undetected within the movement for so many years. The suspicion will be that there are touts operating in every crevice of the IRA. However, that would not be accurate. Yes, they are penetrated, but that should come as no surprise. It is the depth of penetration that has caused the high level of concern. The perception which was always prevalent within the movement was that if you got your hands dirty – ie, hands-on killing – you were clean. This was the single most damaging assumption the movement made in the present campaign. This assumption was played upon by the security forces. I suppose the belief was that even the Brits wouldn't allow people to get away with murder, especially multiple murders. How wrong can one be?

✶ ✶ ✶

On the evening of Easter Monday, 20 April 1987, Inspector Dave Ead was checking on his foot patrols around the seaside town of Newcastle, County Down. Happy with the way the massive crowds and the traffic they brought with them were being supervised, he decided to return to the town's police station. He walked along the promenade, thronged with families enjoying the rare sunny day. Two gunmen walked up behind him and fired a number of shots into his back. He fell to the ground, mortally wounded, as children all around screamed. In the confusion the gunmen made their escape, running to a motorbike and fleeing the town.

Inspector Ead, originally from Plymouth, England, had joined the RUC in 1970. He was promoted to inspector in 1982 and the following year escaped a bomb attack on the university at Jordanstown, County Antrim, which left three fellow officers dead. In 1994 Ead's widow told a BBC documentary of the day her husband died: 'It was a gorgeous day, Easter Monday. This place was black with people. It was crowded. Everybody was down at the seaside; and to think that when so many people are here to enjoy themselves that there was somebody in the crowd who was out just with one purpose, and that was to kill a police officer. I was ironing and a police officer's wife arrived and I took her upstairs to see a new bedroom unit. We were just upstairs when crowds of people came to the door and then the police officer's wife said to me, "Christine, David's dead." My two girls were in bed and they are normally not very good sleepers, but they did sleep that night. And when I told them the next morning, it's just something I will never forget. Our home has lost all the fun and happiness. There's times I feel awfully guilty and I think really, my girls, for a lot of their childhood, really I have been mourning Dave's death and maybe I haven't at times been enough fun, whereas Dave had a good sense of humour and our home was happy.'

When Dave Ead was murdered he left behind two doting daughters, aged eleven and nine. In January 2000, Mrs Ead spoke to the *Daily Mirror*'s Jilly Beattie about the changing of the name of the RUC to the PSNI and the Patten reforms. Mrs Ead said: 'I am brokenhearted by the betrayal of the good men and women of the RUC and their families. Of course we want to live in a society where our officers do not need to carry guns. We want to live in a society where the families of officers do not have to live behind bulletproof windows and check under their car every time they use it. We want to feel safe and free from the terror which has plagued us for more than thirty years. But to change the name and insignia of the RUC is an insult and a betrayal. It dishonours the officers who have given their lives to the protection of entire communities. It dishonours the men and women disabled and disfigured by terrorist atrocities. It dishonours the families of every RUC officer, alive and dead. Changing the name suggests that they have not been honourable in their jobs, that somehow we should be ashamed of the name of the RUC. My husband was murdered by the IRA, but I didn't just lose the man I loved – I lost everything and so did our daughters, Deborah and Lorna. But even before David was killed, we had sacrificed so much for his job. We lost our freedom and our sense of safety because of his job. I have shed so many tears over the years that I thought I had none left. But I have shed tears over the Patten Report. I am sickened by this. But there is one thing that they can't take away and that is the fact that I am – and always will be – an RUC widow.'

The real betrayal however did not lie with Chris Patten, most of whose reforms the British Government later implemented. The true betrayal lies with those in the security forces who knew, and still know, that the IRA member who supplied the gun and the motorbike for the murder of Dave Ead was an agent; and that one of the two gunmen who shot him to death and deprived two young girls of their dad was also an agent of the security forces. This is what happened in Northern Ireland during the real dirty war. Lines got blurred. People were sacrificed to save agents. Dave Ead was one such sacrifice.

We have established that while CID officers did all they could to bring the killers to justice, they were never told the perpetrators were on their side. Agent involvement in murder was widespread throughout the Troubles. Agents could not operate properly without killing. Yes, they saved many lives, but at the expense of others. Little wonder then that the clear-up rate in bringing killers before the courts was so appallingly bad over the past thirty years. So many of those killers, both loyalist and republican, were also working for the security forces.

The final chapter on those who died during the Troubles has yet to be written. When it is, perhaps one question in the conclusion will be this: who really ran the Troubles?

❋ ❋ ❋

My relationship with the Stevens Inquiry was to change when a former member of the FRU began to circulate e-mails about my true identity and details regarding my family to a number of media outlets. These e-mails were signed 'Friends of the FRU'. I acquired copies of these e-mails and supplied them to Stevens. Initially Stevens appeared keen and willing to investigate. After approximately three weeks the e-mails were traced to a computer belonging to a former work colleague who himself wrote a book entitled, *Fishers of Men*, using the pseudonym of Rob Lewis – a book that was approved for publication by the Ministry of Defence. The computer was taken away to be investigated, the individual admitted his role in sending these e-mails and initially it appeared the case was proceeding well, like any case of intimidation against a police witness. A member of the Stevens Inquiry told me that this individual's phone records showed that he had been in contact with other members of the FRU, both serving and past. Given the slow and deliberate pace at which Sir John Stevens normally operates his inquiries, I was amazed when after only one month a decision was taken to drop the charges against the individual on the advice of the crown prosecution service. To say that I was annoyed is an understatement.

As a direct consequence, in consultation with my wife, I withdrew my cooperation with Sir John Stevens and his inquiry after three separate days of giving evidence. My wife had initially been reassured by the inquiry team, prior to me making any statement, that, should my statement to Sir John's inquiry cause a negative reaction from my former colleagues, we would be 'protected'. An affidavit sworn by a senior MOD official stated clearly and unequivocally: 'If identified, both a past and serving member of the FRU are liable to be captured and interrogated, tortured and murdered by Republican terrorist organisations. Those who are no longer serving in the unit also require protection, especially if they have since left the armed forces. When they are separated from the protection of military institutions, they and their family are more vulnerable to terrorist attacks'. The argument that was being presented to me and being used against me in court procedures was exactly the threat against a possible exposure. Here we had direct evidence of an individual breaching the same Official Secrets Act that was being used against me but, for whatever reason, the British State decided that both myself and my family did not warrant their protection. Imagine telling your wife that. I had already been arrested and questioned over allegations that I had been speaking to the media, that I was the whistleblower behind certain newspaper articles. I was accused of breaching the Official Secrets Act. Documents stolen from my home were produced in the case against me. It was incredible. I am now banned from talking about the FRU to anyone other than the Stevens Inquiry.

These attempts to intimidate and silence me continued in other ways. Personal details were leaked to certain journalists, details which could only have come from the Ministry of Defence. I do not intend at this stage to outline all of the methods of intimidation used against me to stop me becoming a whistleblower but if you are reading this book and I am still alive then I count my blessings.

In some ways I am pleased that I no longer have contact with the Stevens team, as to date I have seen nothing that would reassure me that this inquiry was anything other than a vehicle for delay. I take no satisfaction from saying that, but the death of Stobie, the arrest of Barrett and the timing of subsequent charges and, most important, the failure to make any arrest or press charges against any serving or past members of the FRU or RUC is hard to justify.

Since I withdrew my statement and cooperation from the Stevens team I have had no further dealings with them. Society is not yet ready to protect whistleblowers, and your life is definitely in danger if you are a whistleblower who worked for the security services in Northern Ireland. I have no doubt about that. But I also believe that those families who lost loved ones in the Troubles, whether as a result of actions by the State or by other paramilitary organisations, deserve action and answers. That is why I have tried where possible to help the families who lost relatives on Bloody Sunday as well as the families of Pat Finucane and Francisco Notorantonio. In the latter two cases I believe it may be many years before the families are finally given the truth. As long as the British government fails to protect those who try to search for the truth, others will be discouraged from coming forward. At the time of writing I am encouraged by the fact that other intelligence service operatives are now considering coming forward. Time will tell.

Glossary

AWOL Absent without leave

CF Contact Form. Records all meetings with agents

CID Criminal Intelligence Division

CLF Commander Land Forces

CO Commanding Officer

DSF Director of Special Forces

DUP Democratic Unionist Party

FRU Force Research Unit

HQNI British Army Headquarters Northern Ireland (also FRU operations office)

INLA Irish National Liberation Army, founded in 1974 as a split from the official IRA

IO Intelligence officer

IRA Irish Republican Army. Used in the book to refer to the Provisional IRA (PIRA)

JSG Joint Services Group (formerly FRU)

MI5 Military Intelligence 5. The Security Service. Britain's domestic military intelligence agency

MI6 Military Intelligence 6. The Secret Intelligence Service. Britain's foreign military intelligence agency

MISR Military Intelligence Source Report

MOD Ministry Of Defence

MRF Mobile Reconnaissance Force

OTR An 'On the Run' terrorist

PLO Palestine Liberation Organisation

PUP Progressive Unionist Party. Formed in 1979. Political wing of outlawed UVF

PSNI Police Service of Northern Ireland (formerly RUC)

ROI Republic of Ireland

RUC Royal Ulster Constabulary (now PSNI)

SAS Special Air Service

SDLP Social Democratic Labour Party

SF Sinn Féin

SIW Special Intelligence Wing

SPV Special patrol vehicles – all vehicles used by the FRU

TCG Tasking and Coordinating Group

UDA Ulster Defence Association. Largest loyalist paramilitary group, formed in 1971

UDR Ulster Defence Regiment (now Royal Irish Rangers)

UFF Ulster Freedom Fighters. Cover name for the UDA

UPVF Ulster Protestant Volunteer Force

UVF Ulster Volunteer Force. Loyalist paramilitary group formed in 1966

VCP Vehicle Check Point (IVCP Illegal checkpoint operated by paramilitaries)

West Det. FRU's western detachment, so East Det., etc.